Theology and Pastoral Care

Creative Pastoral Care and Counseling Series
    Editor: Howard J. Clinebell, Jr.
    Associate Editor: Howard W. Stone

The Care and Counseling of Youth in the Church by Paul B. Irwin
*Growth Counseling for Marriage Enrichment: Pre-Marriage and the
    Early Years* by Howard J. Clinebell, Jr.
Crisis Counseling by Howard W. Stone
Pastoral Counseling in Grief and Separation by Wayne E. Oates
Counseling for Liberation by Charlotte Holt Clinebell
Growth Counseling for Mid-Years Couples by Howard J. Clinebell, Jr.
Theology and Pastoral Care by John B. Cobb, Jr.

Theology and
Pastoral Care

John B. Cobb, Jr.

Fortress Press   Philadelphia

Library of Congress Catalog Card Number 76–007862
ISBN 0–8006–0557–8

5768G76   Printed in U.S.A.   1–557

Contents

Series Foreword

Let me share with you some of the hopes that are in the minds of those of us who helped to develop this series—hopes that relate directly to you as the reader. It is our desire and expectation that these books will be of help to you in developing better working tools as a minister-counselor. We hope that they will do this by encouraging your own creativity in developing more effective methods and programs for helping people live life more fully. It is our intention in this series to affirm the many things you have going for you as a minister in helping troubled persons—the many assets and resources from your religious heritage, your role as the leader of a congregation, and your unique relationship to individuals and families throughout the life cycle. We hope to help you reaffirm the *power of the pastoral* by the use of fresh models and methods in your ministry.

The aim of the series is not to be comprehensive with respect to topics but rather to bring innovative approaches to some major types of counseling. Although the books are practice-oriented, they also provide a solid foundation of theological and psychological insights. They are written primarily for ministers (and those preparing for the ministry) but we hope that they will also prove useful to other counselors who are interested in the crucial role of spiritual and value issues in all helping relationships. In addition we hope that the series will be useful in seminary courses, clergy support groups, continuing education workshops, and lay befriender training.

This is a period of rich new developments in counseling and psychotherapy. The time is ripe for a flowering of creative methods and insights in pastoral care and counseling. Our expectation is that this series will stimulate grass-roots creativity as innovative methods and programs come alive for you. Some of the major thrusts that will be discussed in this series include a new awareness of the unique contributions of the theologically trained counselor, the liberating power of the human potentials orientation, an appreciation of the pastoral-care function of the ministering congregation, the importance of humanizing systems and institutions as well as close relationships, the importance of pastoral *care* (and not just counseling), the many opportunities for caring ministries throughout the life cycle, the deep changes in male-female relationships, and the new psychotherapies such as Gestalt therapy, Transactional Analysis, educative counseling, and crisis methods. Our hope is that this series will enhance your resources for your ministry to persons by opening doorways to understanding of these creative thrusts in pastoral care and counseling.

In this volume John B. Cobb, Jr., a distinguished theologian, reflects on the challenge of utilizing the riches of the Christian heritage more effectively in caring and counseling. In these times of spiritual search and value hunger the integration of theology in the practice of ministry is an urgent need. This integration is particularly crucial in the practice of pastoral care as we struggle to define our distinctive contribution to the growth and healing of persons.

John Cobb gives us here a valuable resource for this integrative task. Beginning with an understanding of the nature of Christian existence, he draws implications for the life of the church in general and for pastoral care in particular. Many of his key concepts will be both illuminating and functional for pastoral counselors. I found myself resonating to his definition of health as "inclusive wholeness centering in spirit" and his view of the church as "a mutually participating community of self-transcending selves." One of the distinctive strengths of his book is that he tackles the difficult (and risky) task of applying his working concepts to concrete pastoral counseling relationships.

It has been my privilege to know John Cobb as a friend and colleague for some nineteen years. As will be evident to the reader, he brings to the writing of this volume an incisive, gifted mind. Equally important, he also brings warm-hearted caring and sensitive awareness of human beings. These qualities make him a natural counselor and pastor to many of us whose lives are touched by his.

This book will be both a confronting challenge and a significant resource to pastors and to other counselors who see the growth of *spiritual* wholeness as an essential goal in their work with people. It will help us facilitate the process by which, in the author's words, "a sense of God's effective presence moves to the heart of the counseling situation."

HOWARD J. CLINEBELL, JR.

Preface

Christian faith is relevant to every aspect of life. It has particular relevance for the church and its activities, and therefore for pastors who have special responsibility for the appropriateness of these activities. Theology is the articulation of faith, and hence professional theologians, as those charged to lead in this articulation, should assist pastors in fulfilling their responsibilities. But in recent decades things have not worked out in this way.

Pastors have received some help from professional theologians in their role as preachers, but very little in their other roles. They have turned elsewhere, and often humanistic psychologists have become their theological guides for pastoral care and counseling. Since humanistic psychology has deep roots in Jewish and Christian traditions, pastors have been able to appropriate from it without abandoning their Christian faith. Still there is danger that the center will not hold, that the several roles of the pastor will lose their unity, and that the total life of the church will not be informed by what is distinctive in the Christian faith.

There is no quick and easy solution to this problem. It is a sign of progress when a professional theologian is asked to contribute to a series on pastoral care and counseling, but the results also highlight the problems on both sides. On the side of theology, only *a* Christian theology can be presented in its possible relevance for the work of pastors. On the side of pastoral care, the series as a whole will be little affected by the understanding of Christian faith here offered. The bridge is still lacking.

Nevertheless, I appreciate the openness of the editors of this series that allows me, as a professional theologian, to enter into the discussion. The selected theological ideas I have offered are more fully developed elsewhere, especially in my *The Structure of Christian Existence* and *God and the World*. In the present book I have stated these ideas very briefly so as to leave space to deal explicitly with their implications for pastoral care and counseling.

Counseling and theology have best been brought together in the past in the area of the understanding of love and acceptance. This is an important topic and is worthy of renewed statement and emphasis. However, because it has been extensively discussed elsewhere, I have used my limited space for other topics. This has led me to a quite one-sided discussion of God in chapter 4. For Christian faith God is not only the "directivity" there described but also the one who accepts us no matter how we respond to that directivity. Two books can be especially recommended to those who want to pursue this topic: Thomas C. Oden's *Kerygma and Counseling* and Don Browning's *Atonement and Psychotherapy*.

Both of the editors of this series have given valuable help in the writing of this book. In addition I am particularly indebted for wise counsel and practical assistance to Scott Sullender and Gordon Jackson.

Theology and Pastoral Care

1. Theology, Pastoral Counseling, and Pastoral Care

The academic disciplines of theology and pastoral counseling have too long been at odds. In many seminary faculties their representatives have been suspicious of one another. Professors of theology have suspected that the beliefs that inform the teaching of counseling are not clearly Christian, that they have been derived from secular psychology and only superficially adapted for pastoral use. Professors of pastoral counseling have suspected that most of what takes place in courses on theology is irrelevant to meeting the human needs the minister is called upon to address. Unfortunately, both suspicions are too well-founded.

The time is now propitious to work toward a new relation between these disciplines. On the one side, the theological chaos of the last decade expressed the determination of theologians to deal more concretely with the realities of our human situation. On the other side, pastoral counselors are increasingly concerned to establish and clarify their distinctive contribution and role as pastors and as Christians.

Theological Definitions of the Minister's Task

Wanting a more fruitful relationship is the first step toward *achieving* it, but only the first step. Goodwill and theological study help, but there is a deeper obstacle to the mutual fructification of theology and counseling. There is a tension between the assumptions built into the usual counseling model and the implications of most theology for the pastoral ministry. For example, much theology calls for ministers to be custodians and proclaimers of a Word entrusted to them, whereas the one-to-one relation in the counselor's office is a poor place for this. Other theologies point toward leadership of a congregation in its corporate life and its service to the world as the minister's central task, whereas therapeutic assistance to individuals is peripheral to that form of ministry. Other theologies see the minister as primarily a priest mediating between the divine and the human through a sacramental ministry, whereas pastoral counseling is not sacramental in any obvious sense. Still other theologies stress the importance of Christian identification with the poor, the disfranchised, and the oppressed, whereas most counselees are of the middle class.

Even when a theology does stress the importance of pastoral ministry to individuals in their individual needs, the definition of these needs is likely to be quite different. For example, some theologians imply that the minister should guide the members of the congregation into a deeper understanding and appropriation of the gospel. This would be done in part on a one-to-one basis, and it casts the minister in the role of spiritual director. But the role of spiritual director is different from that of counselor, and even from pastoral care as usually understood and practiced. In many segments of our society those seeking religious direction are more likely to go to humanistic psychologists, Jungian analysts, or Indian gurus than to Christian ministers trained as pastoral counselors.

Nevertheless, no adequate account of the role of ministers can exclude their counseling of those who come to them with urgently felt needs. Human needs make a claim upon the church. It is appropriate that persons who suffer turn to the church's professional leadership for help, just as the physically sick and mentally disturbed turned to Jesus. At times he avoided the pressure of their demands for healing so as to devote his time and energy to teaching about the coming kingdom, but healing was also an important part of his minis-

try.   Responding to the suffering caused by the structures of
the present age was secondary to his work of ushering in the
new age, but, as secondary, it was still important.

Theology and Counseling

The recognition by theologians of the validity of counseling
as part of the minister's task is a second step toward achieving
a more fruitful relationship between theology and the pastor's
role as counselor.   But this second step only prepares us to
ask whether theology has anything to say that is relevant to the
actual work of pastoral counseling.   Thus far it has said very
little.   Paul Tillich's theology has been congenial to pastoral
counseling because of his association of Christian salvation
with healing, his sensitivity to psychotherapy, and his interpretation of justification by faith as accepting one's acceptance.   Tillich's theology has in these ways built bridges of
understanding and reassured pastors as to the Christian substance of their counseling.   But it is not clear that pastors
have learned much from him that informs the counseling itself.

When the basic model of counseling is therapy as defined by
other professions, it seems that counseling by pastors does not
vary much from other counseling.   There are particular in-
stances in which pastors are sensitized to aspects of a counselee's problem by their theological preparation, and counseling
by pastors is often affected by their understanding of their role
as ministers.   When the Christian faith gives pastors an assurance of God's grace and of the meaningfulness of life, this
assurance is subtly communicated to their counselees.   When
their Christian experience has made them deeply loving persons, their love is in itself therapeutic.   When belief in God
leads to assurance that no one is beyond redemption, the pastor may have hope where other counselors despair.   But
theology has little to say about the goals and methods of this
kind of counseling except that they too are legitimate if they
ease suffering and restore community.

Perhaps we should be satisfied with these limited relations.

If the church provides a gymnasium for the young people of the community and the minister coaches the basketball team, we do not ask theologians to do more than explain why this is an appropriate expression of Christian ministry. We hope that the minister's Christian concern will help the youth grow, but we do not look for a theology of coaching. When we send medical missionaries to parts of the world where they are needed, we do not ask them to practice distinctively Christian medicine. We think that the personal commitment and human concern of these doctors will enhance their effectiveness, but we do not need to introduce specifically theological considerations. Why should we expect more of theology when the therapy we offer is psychological instead of physical? We want the minister who coaches basketball to be a good coach, and the medical missionary to be a good doctor, but we leave the definition of excellence in these areas to others. Is it not enough that the pastoral counselor be a good counselor by the norms that are recognized in all counseling professions?

The problem with these analogies is that they refer to activities recognized as peripheral to the pastor's role, whereas counseling is viewed as central. If it is central, then it must be a vital part of pastoral care in general, and the whole of pastoral care should be theologically informed.

This means that the practice of counseling by pastors should be seen not only as one expression of Christian concern to respond to human needs in general but also as a part of the distinctive pastoral work of making Christian faith effective in the lives of people. Here lies the challenge. Can pastors bring their faith to bear on the goals, methods, and resources of counseling? Is there a type of counseling that is given distinctive shape and direction not only by the pastor's socially defined role but also by Christian understanding of God and the world?

Before attempting a systematic account of how Christian theology is now, or might be, expressed and communicated in pastoral care and counseling, we will consider a specific instance of such counseling. Examination of this instance can clarify the difference between counseling as ministry to human need in general and counseling as making Christian faith effective. On that basis the agenda for the remaining chapters of the book can be presented.

Chester Carter and Pastor Jones

Pastor Jones heard that Chester Carter was in the hospital for minor surgery. Carter was a fifty-five-year-old man, married for twenty-five years, and the father of three children, all of whom were married or living on their own. He worked as an accounting clerk for a large insurance firm in town. He had recently moved into the area, and soon after he came he joined Pastor Jones's church. Mrs. Carter did not join, and she seldom accompanied him to church affairs. Pastor Jones called on the Carters in their home and had amiable but superficial talks with both of them. Mrs. Carter explained that she had never been a churchgoing person.

In the hospital Chester seemed particularly pleased to have the chance to talk. He told his pastor that he had been trying to muster the courage to make an appointment to see him. Even on the first visit, soon after the operation, Chester talked freely of his fears about his work. Since college he had been "canned" from some twenty jobs, mostly because he could not get along with his bosses (men). But he liked his present job because he felt little pressure from superiors and enjoyed the presence of attractive younger women in the office. He did not want to lose this job.

Pastor Jones returned to see Chester the next day. Chester was stronger, and Pastor Jones encouraged him to share more deeply. Chester was worried because he would get "crushes" on young, attractive women, especially his office coworkers. He felt attraction toward these young women and fantasized about possible romances and sexual adventures. He was easily hurt and became deeply depressed when he sensed rejection from one of these office crushes. He felt repelled by women of his own age, including his wife. But, since he did not know how to get appropriately close to younger women either, he spent many a coffee break and lunch period alone. He also had difficulty relating to men who were his superiors in the office. He wondered if all this was "normal."

As they talked further, Pastor Jones learned more of Chester's background. His relationship with his father had never been close. He saw his father as a loner who argued and shouted a lot. Though he had a closer relationship with his mother, she had a violent temper and he was sometimes the object of "heavy beatings." He remembered her crying when he refused to kiss her goodbye anymore as he left for elementary school. He said he was too embarrassed. During school years he was shy and had few friends, but did well academically.

Pastor Jones was curious about Mrs. Carter. Chester spoke of their having been "on the verge of divorce" ever since they got married. He was "repulsed" by her and could touch her only when they were trying to "have sex." Furthermore, he confessed to being impotent with her when they tried. He masturbated daily. He felt that she was constantly criticizing him for the way he ate, dressed, drove—everything. He complained that she did not socialize enough and was overweight.

Pastor Jones was a little overwhelmed by Chester's confession. He did his best to hear him out with sympathy and acceptance, but he had little immediate response. Later that week, as Pastor Jones thought about Chester's story, he was struck by Chester's fear of intimate relationships. Even his crushes on unavailable women seemed to keep him at a distance, thus protecting him from emotional intimacy. So also, his marital relationship and the lack of interest in people his own age seemed to keep him lonely, a position that was probably safer for him than being close to another person. He did not want to see himself as a fifty-five-year-old man, preferring instead to see himself as the type of person who just might one day hit it off with a young, attractive woman. On the one hand he expressed the pain and fear of his lonely lifestyle, yet on the other hand his obsessions and his marital style prevented him from establishing healthy relations.

It was clear that Chester wanted help from Pastor Jones, but what kind of help? On his next visit Pastor Jones kept prodding for an answer to that question, but Chester either could not or would not make clear what he wanted. Pastor Jones felt that he could not help Chester much until he knew what Chester really wanted. He began to think that what Chester wanted was help in establishing a successful relationship with one of his young female coworkers.

Pastor Jones worried about the deep-seated psychological problems that Chester revealed to him, and on their last visit together he suggested to Chester that he enter a therapy group led by a psychologist in town. Chester agreed. This was a group for men only, mostly men in their middle years, who would meet at regular intervals to share their problems and support one another. Pastor Jones hoped this might give Chester an opportunity to break out of his lonely lifestyle and learn the skills of friendship. He hoped that by gradually trusting a caring community Chester might share some of his inner world and, perhaps for the first time, experience acceptance and grace.

Some Theological Reflections

Pastor Jones undoubtedly performed a Christian ministry for Chester Carter. By visiting him in the hospital he was making effective and appropriate use of his special role as pastor. Pastors can take this kind of initiative in relation to people who need help, whereas most other counseling professions are not able to do so. Since Chester needed help and Pastor Jones was the one in the best position to help, we can be grateful that he made himself available. Further, Chester would not have spoken so freely of his problems had not his pastor communicated openness and concern for him.

But beyond this point there was little that is distinctively pastoral or Christian in the way Pastor Jones dealt with Chester Carter. The problem was to be defined by the counselee's felt needs, and insofar as the pastor's judgment of what was needed comes into play it has to do with satisfying human relationships. Concern for Chester's own definition of his problem and for his attainment of satisfying human relationships was fully appropriate from a Christian point of view. But Christianity also confronts us with a challenge to our own definitions of our needs, and there is much more to the Christian understanding of human fulfillment. Pastor Jones undoubtedly knew this, and probably his preaching was informed by an understanding of his prophetic mission and a fuller appreciation of what was involved in Christian life. But there was no indication that this knowledge affected his response to Chester. In chapter 2 some specific suggestions will be made as to what more Pastor Jones might have done. These will be set in the context of an effort to define the spirit as what is distinctive to Christian existence. In chapter 3 this distinctive Christian element will be set in the context of a wholistic view of Christian existence, and suggestions made as to the possible implications for pastoral care.

Pastor Jones undoubtedly was motivated to help Chester by a deep faith in God. However, there was nothing in this account to indicate how that faith affected the counselor's actual responses and suggestions to the counselee. This is not a criticism of Pastor Jones, but it is a commentary on our time that in the relation of this pastor to his parishioner's acute personal problem, faith in God must remain in the background, unexpressed. Chapter 4 will propose a way of thinking about God that is concretely related to ordinary experience, in the hope that this may help pastors articulate the relevance of their faith. It will also suggest ways in which this understanding of God can affect pastoral care.

What is lacking is not only talk about God but the language of faith generally. Undoubtedly that language is used by both

Chester Carter and Pastor Jones as they worship together on Sunday mornings. But there seems to be little carry-over to the discussion of the critical issues of daily life. Chapter 5 will discuss this problem and suggest a direction. Rather than exhort or complain, it will conclude with a fictional story designed to show how a few elements of traditional Christian language can reenter our vocabulary in a way that illumines our real experience. This story will also illustrate the results of thinking about God in the way proposed in chapter 4.

2. The Human Spirit

There is wide agreement among therapists, counselors, and Christian thinkers that the end toward which we want people to develop is human wholeness. In recent years we have learned that all aspects of our existence interpenetrate one another. We are not a mere composite of separate faculties, and the recognition of this organic character of existence has practical implications. For example, a teacher cannot address the intellect of a child alone, ignoring the whole complex of feelings that support or interfere with the learning process. The teacher should treat the child wholistically as a person. To this insistence on wholeness we will return in chapter 3.

There is danger, however, that this proper stress on the organic unity of human existence may lead us to overlook the distinguishable aspects that are integrated into wholes. We can distinguish the intellectual capacity of the child to learn from the emotional condition of the child which may either support or inhibit learning. Further, not all wholes share all the same aspects. The correct language about indivisible wholes can discourage the important work of analyzing the wholes and developing greater sensitivity to their diversity. Because emotion is the foundational and universal substance of all existence, and because emotional health is, consequently, so important, wholistic thinking has been in danger of identifying "mental health" with emotional health, as if there were no other aspects of existence, or as if these were automatically made healthy by emotional health. As we will see in the next chapter, the encompassing Christian goal for existence includes emotional health as an extremely important ingredient. But the distinctiveness of the Christian goal cannot be explained without distinguishing other aspects of existence from the emotional one. Spirit is that aspect which is decisive for differentiating Christian existence from other forms. This chapter tries to explain what spirit is as an aspect of human existence.

The distinctive aim of the church for individual human beings can be summed up as health and strength of spirit. Worship and preaching are major ways in which the church strengthens the spirit. But the whole of pastoral care, including counseling, can contribute to this goal. Suggestions will be offered in the pages that follow concerning how the goal of strengthening the human spirit can inform pastoral care and counseling.

Spirit as Self-Transcending Selfhood

The spirit is the self or "I." It is the center within the psychic life in terms of which the whole is organized. Some aspects of that life may be experienced as threatening or alien or as means to be employed for one's purposes. The self is the point of reference for these evaluations. One may "use" one's reason or "control" one's emotions. One *is* one's self or spirit.

But not every self or "I" is spirit. The account of Chester in chapter 1 suggested that his life may be organized around his desire for intimacy with young women. This consuming drive thus constitutes his selfhood as the organizing center of his existence. Chester might be asking the pastor to help him realize this self rather than to overcome that self-identification in favor of one the counselor regards more highly. The self may then be a strong, emotional desire, and when this is the case, the self is not spirit. Under these circumstances spirit is lacking.

The self is spirit only when the self as the organizing center transcends the emotions and other aspects of the psychic life. When Chester can see that his emotional desire for sexual intimacy with young women is an impediment to his true self-realization, then his self will transcend that desire. That transcendence *could* be simply in terms of another, stronger desire, for example, to maintain a respectable image. In that case spirit is not involved. But it could also be in terms of a center that transcends all his desires and evaluates them in relation to ends that they do not establish. In that case spirit would be present.

Spirit not only transcends emotional desires, it also transcends itself. "Transcends" here means "looks at" and "takes responsibility for." The spiritual person can take a look at herself or himself and take responsibility for what she or he sees. But the *self*-transcendent self takes responsibility for itself, including its attitude toward the other aspects of the psychic life. It cannot finally be detached.

Among many of those who seek help through counseling, spirit is weak or absent. Examination of another example will help to highlight the nature and importance of spirit.

Brent and Marge

Pastor Scott was surprised to see Brent and Marge. Marge's parents had been members of the church for a while, and Marge had been in Sunday school for a few years. Brent had come occasionally to the high school group, but his parents were poor and moved often. Pastor Scott had officiated at their wedding four years earlier, but he had not seen them since.

Now, in their late twenties, they returned for marriage counseling. Apparently they had no one else to whom to turn. Brent had a well-paying job in management in a construction firm. They both complained of a lack of communication and a lack of common interests in their marriage, but their most pressing concern was Marge's current affair with another man, who was also married. They were confused and upset, feeling their marriage crashing on the rocks below them. They wanted to see if Pastor Scott could help.

As they talked together, Marge expressed ambivalent feelings about the affair and the marriage, but was willing to try to work on the marriage. Brent wanted very much to keep Marge and the marriage, and was willing to accept the pastor's suggestions. Brent also seemed willing to admit some of his mistakes. He identified his preoccupation with his work and his inability to know how to treat Marge as a person as possible reasons why Marge had sought another man.

While Brent and Marge knew each other in high school, they first met in a romantic way only six months before they got married. After the wedding Marge quit work, expecting children. The children never came, and tensions grew, compounded by hurt feelings and mutual accusations. Their four years of marriage were characterized by extensive social activities, with frequent trips across the country, to Europe, and to other distant places. Their social-recreational life seemed centered around being entertained by a third element (travel, the Club) rather than around doing simple things together.

Pastor Scott was concerned about Marge's ambivalence, wondering if she really did want to save the marriage. He therefore suggested a plan of five conjoint counseling sessions, to be followed by a reevaluation of motivations and goals.

To Pastor Scott there seemed to be a war going on between Brent and Marge. This unacknowledged warfare was reflected in their mutual mistrust, the sexual acting out, and a general competitiveness over household jobs, among other things. He was also struck by the general lack of communication skills, including the inability to talk intimately with each other about feelings of tenderness and pain.

As the three of them worked together over the weeks, Marge seemed concerned about the ethics of her decision. She was caught between her husband and that other man, not knowing which she wanted. But in the midst of all this was her own emerging identity too. Where could she be a person? And with whom?

Brent also came to be increasingly in touch with his values. He knew that he wanted to be rich, live comfortably, belong to the Club, and have a pretty wife. Those things were most important to him. He was dealing with the pressure by drinking, golf, and general avoidance. But now he feared he would lose his wife.

After five sessions, some progress was made in communicating and clarifying issues. Marge came to the important decision that she wanted the other man more. This was too painful for Brent, and he tried to persuade her to just try a separation for now, to give them more time to work it out. But from Marge's point of view she needed more time alone, on her own, away from Brent. And for her, this meant terminating counseling.

So Brent and Marge ended their contact with Pastor Scott. He was glad to have helped, if only temporarily. But what bothered him most was his feeling of helplessness in the face of the issues of ethics and values with which this couple struggled. Without a common theological language and an ongoing pastoral relationship, it seemed difficult to offer much guidance.

Some Theological Comments

Brent appeared to have a strong self in the sense of definite controlling desires which governed everything else. He was determined to be rich, live comfortably, belong to the Club, and have a pretty wife. Presumably these were the kinds of achievements that were admired in the circle in which he moved, so we may assume that at a deeper level his desire was to be successful in the eyes of his peers. To achieve this success he wanted to hold onto his wife and hence was open to working on the relationship. But there was little indication of transcendence over the desires themselves.

Marge appeared to have a weaker self in the sense that her central point of reference was not so fixed or clear. She did not quite know what she wanted and, therefore, who she was. That she considered the question of right and wrong indicated that there was some tendency to transcend her desires, but apparently this was not strongly established. It was perhaps only a case of conflicting desires, her desire to have her own approval and that of other people being at odds with her desire for her lover. Perhaps Marge's desire for fuller personhood introduced a thrust toward transcendence.

Taking Brent as the clearer instance, we can see that at this level of existence the meaning and purpose of life is not in question. The admiration of his peers sets the context for Brent's efforts to succeed. To achieve what is admired is self-evidently worthwhile. The problem is only to attain what is valued by his peers. If Brent gained transcendence over his present desires, they would appear extremely problematic and no longer be evident to him as worth attaining. The problem of meaning would be opened up. He would then begin a new struggle to discover what ends are truly worthwhile or what style of life is actually fulfilling or appropriate. Approaches and solutions of the great philosophies and religions would then become relevant. In short, his selfhood would become spirit.

Insofar as one accepts a meaning for life, one judges one's life by that meaning. One aspires to be what one is not. This is quite different from desire. We *desire* to gain ends that are set by our emotions. But our spiritual aspirations are for the change of our desires. Our aspirations have to do with what in our very selfhood we believe we should become. They deal with the motivations of our actions. For example, we may aspire to become people who act out of disinterested love for others rather than out of emotional desires.

Such disinterested love is possible in principle only at the level of spirit. Insofar as the self is its desires, love is a form of desire and is governed by the attractiveness of the object. But when the self transcends the desires, and itself also, then one element among its complex purposes may be for the well-being of others as well as itself. This element is not governed by the attractiveness of those whose well-being is intended. Also, in principle, it is possible for this element in the intention to transcend any expectation of benefit to the self.

The purposes of spirit can also lead to commitment in a very different sense from what is possible for Brent. Brent was committed to success in the eyes of his peers, and he was willing to make sacrifices in order to fulfill this commitment. But at the level of spirit, commitment can be to purposes that are freely chosen and are not self-regarding. One may be committed to peace, to the church, or to the advancement of knowledge. These commitments are in danger of being idolatrous if they block openness to the fresh directivity of God. But if they express that directivity in the concrete situation in which one finds oneself, they are a part of healthy spiritual life.

The commitments of the spirit express an additional aspect of what is meant by self-transcendence. The ability to transcend one's personal self means that one views oneself as an individual self among others. Disinterested concern for other selves as well as for oneself follows as the appropriate response to this self-transcending perspective. It does not for that reason immediately become actual, so that the aspiration to disinterested concern remains in tension with the self's exaggerated concern for itself. But the aspiration is not without effect.

Spiritual life is not always healthy. The ability to transcend oneself and to take responsibility for oneself can lead to paralyzing guilt or to preoccupation with one's own virtue or salvation. The question of meaning can be asked without finding an answer, or with an answer that distorts the aspirations and commitments that follow from it. These problems are absent from Brent's life. For spiritual life the stakes are higher, the need for mutual support is greater, the dangers of perversion are more serious. Above all, the spiritual life can be healthy only as it is grounded in the assurance of an acceptance that no human being can give, the ultimate acceptance that is God's.

The Church and the Spirit

If health and strength of spirit is the central distinctive goal of Christian life, then the whole work of the church should be guided by this goal. The church can confront us with an ideal for our existence that is in tension with our emotional desires. It can enlist our desires through creating a climate of admiration for this ideal, so that our desire to be admired by others encourages us to accept and attempt to embody the ideal. The resulting aspiration cuts itself free from the desire that supports it; for the ideal includes freedom from control by the admiration of others.

The tension between the ideal to which we aspire and our ordinary desires produces, itself, a transcendence over those desires. We cannot identify ourselves with desires that we do not fully approve. We are encouraged to reflect on the extent to which we really aspire to be what we are not and the extent to which our actual motivations correspond with what we aspire to be. Thus we are encouraged to take responsibility for what we are.

At the same time we are surrounded in the church by the assurance that God loves us whether or not we succeed in becoming what we are called to be. Normatively, the fellowship of the church gives some embodiment to this forgiving and accepting love of God. Thus as we enter into spiritual existence we are given the possibility of being free from the enervating preoccupation with ourselves that is the spirit's peculiar perversion. Also, the church brings its accumulated wisdom to bear in helping us with the understanding of the meaning of our existence—a question to which our self-transcendence radically introduces us. All this the church accomplishes through its central life of worship and its study of the Bible.

However, in recent times, unclarity about purposes, alienation from the Bible, and boredom with worship have combined to weaken the capacity of the church to encourage its people to enter into spiritual existence. When the church becomes conventional, or when it adapts New Testament ideals to what is comfortable and convenient in the society, or when it substitutes for the impossible claims of the Christian ideal of pure disinterested love a system of possible rules, spiritual existence is no longer encouraged. To reconstitute the church as a community that evokes and strengthens spirit requires more than the effort to reinvigorate worship and Bible study. The full range of pastoral care is called into play.

Small Groups for Strengthening the Spirit

One important instrument of pastoral care is the small group. Small groups can be organized for the purpose of encouraging spirit in ways that are more self-conscious and direct than the traditional means of the church. This is not to be taken for granted, however, as the normal function of a small group in the church. Most of the small groups inspired by secular psychological movements neglect the spirit. For example, they often do not encourage the expression of aspirations. In some of these groups, aspirations sound like "pious" concealment of the desires that actually control our actions. In many groups, even in the church, Christians are embarrassed to speak of their nobler aspirations, for example, their desire to be of service to others. Instead they are encouraged to understand and articulate their desires, and even to interpret their aspirations as desires. What we do not speak about, what we do not share, grows weaker. It may fade from our consciousness as we are encouraged to attend to other aspects of the psychic life. Aspiration, unattended to, can die, and with it dies spirit. It is time that the church created more contexts in which, without embarrassment or false piety, Christians can discuss their deepest aspirations, encourage one another in the purification and strengthening of these aspirations, and test their relative success in being transformed in the direction of their aspirations.

The same group that strengthens our aspirations can share in the search for meaning, the examination of motivations, and the testing of commitments. It is even possible to establish groups whose function is to encourage and practice the element of love that can be present in Christian experience. Indeed, we may be grateful that at a time when the traditional forms of the church's life have lost so much of their power, new means of achieving many of the same ends are available. It is important, however, that they be self-consciously chosen, guided by a clear understanding of Christian goals.

Counseling for Growth Toward Spirit

Although counseling is not the major way in which spirit is strengthened and made healthy, and although counseling has other ends that might be thwarted if this one were forced upon it, the pastor who is committed to the encouragement of spirit may find that the practice of conventional counseling is affected by that commitment. It is dangerous to be specific as to what that would entail, but some tentative comments about the stories of Chester (chapter 1) and of Brent and Marge will be suggestive of the kinds of implications this understanding might have for counseling.

In the previous chapter I suggested that Pastor Jones might have responded to Chester Carter in additional ways if the pastor had had in view the distinctively Christian understanding of existence. In the language of this chapter we can say that Chester needed to enter into spiritual existence. If Pastor Jones had approached Chester with this concern, their conversation might have gone somewhat differently. He would have attended not only to Chester's dominant desires for intimacy with young women but also to points in Chester's self-expression where the pastor could detect Chester's rudimentary aspirations to be another kind of person with different desires. Even though this aspiration may have been weaker than the existing desires, it might have been possible to strengthen it by drawing it out, by bringing it more clearly into consciousness, by supporting and encouraging it.

Chester had recently joined the church, and he attended despite his wife's lack of interest. This act alone suggests that there were other sides to Chester's personality. Presumably the purpose of joining was not to increase chances of sexual success with the young women at work. It might have expressed some dim and weak aspiration to find something outside of himself to which he could belong and contribute. Even if it did not, it placed Chester in a context in which such aspirations might be evoked.

The seriousness of Chester's psychological problems may have been such that Pastor Jones was right in wanting him to have professional psychological help. But even if the therapy group were to help Chester to work through his inability to relate to people of his own age and reduce his preoccupation with his present sexual fantasies, the pastor should not be satisfied. Chester needed to view himself and his life in a wider perspective, to see his needs in the context of the needs of others, even those of the whole globe. To help Chester in this direction, the church has resources much better than those of the professional psychologist. Chester can be helped to hear those elements in Pastor Jones's sermons that challenge his preoccupation with himself and his own needs. He can be related to groups in the church that are engaged in service of others as well as mutual help. It may be that involvement with others in such service can create healthy relations with his peers just as effectively as therapy. Perhaps the sexual preoccupations can be lessened as other things take on greater importance in his life. In short, as the self-transcendence that is spirit grows, Chester will be in a better position to deal with the problems that now obsess him.

In the case of Marge, too, there were glimmerings of aspiration that might have been supported and drawn out. She aspired, however fleetingly, to be ethical. I noted above that instead of aspiration this might have been only the desire for approval, but this form of the desire for approval introduces a dynamic of transcendence. To gain approval one must be ethical, but to be ethical is to act without regard for approval. Perhaps the counselor can strengthen whatever tendency exists for moving in this way toward transcendence. Similarly Marge expressed some desire to be a more fully realized person. That also introduces a dynamic of transcendence as the meaning of full humanness is worked out.

Brent gave no sign of aspiration. He seemed settled in his

desires. Apparently in the circles which were important to him success in achieving these desires wins universal approval; there was no indication that these values were freely chosen. Brent's nontranscendent existence depended upon his unanimity of support. Perhaps the counselor is in a position to open Brent to other possibilities. This might be done by frontal attack on his values, that is, by the pastor's communication of the conviction that these are poor and inadequate goals. But a better approach might be to help Brent see that the desire to have a pretty wife for the sake of the admiration of others works against keeping his pretty wife. Here is an avenue to transcendence. Perhaps Brent could be freed to look *at* his desires instead of looking *from* them at the world. In that case a first step toward spirit would be achieved.

Disidentification and the Strengthening of Spirit

It is striking that a method of counseling that is focused on the disengagement of the self from various aspects of the psychic life has become current. That method is Assagioli's psychosynthesis.* It suggests that transcendence of the self over other aspects of the psychic life is the essence of spirit. In such transcendence the "I" objectifies the emotions, the reason, even the will, and thereby distinguishes itself from them.

Two dangers should be kept in mind in the practice of such disidentification. First, the disidentification with other aspects of the psychic life can lead to a denial of responsibility for them. This would move diametrically away from Christian existence in which the objectification is for the purpose of establishing, not one's innocence in relation to what goes on at these levels, but a more radical responsibility. For example, precisely *because* one is not one's emotions, one is responsible for them even beyond one's direct ability to control them or to give them free play. One can adopt the goal of reordering the

---

* For this and all other notes in this book, see the Notes section beginning on p. 75.

emotions to the rest of the psyche so as to change the emotions themselves.

Second, disidentification can lead to the denial of the reality of the self rather than its establishment. If the *I* is not any of these objectifiable activities in the psyche, it may be concluded that the *I* is not at all. But there is a center of consciousness which can be experienced apart from the objectifiable activities of the psyche. The Christian goal is to objectify also this self or *I* that is doing the objectifying, without weakening the sense of the difference. The *I* must learn to accept responsibility for itself.

These cautions are not criticisms of psychosynthesis, which guards against these dangers. They are only reminders that the key work of disidentification is only one side of what is needed. Assagioli provides us with an effective method for strengthening the spirit.

However, the effort to strengthen spirit by itself can have profoundly negative as well as positive consequences. It can proceed at the price of destroying the wholeness of a simpler existence, of thwarting a healthy emotional life, and even of doing injury to the body. Christians have felt that the attainment of self-transcendence has been worth a high price, but the goal cannot be this alone. The full Christian goal is a new wholeness centering in spirit. The following chapter sketches something of what that entails.

3. Christian Wholeness

Having learned that true love for Christ Crucified demands imitation, he decided to conquer his ease-loving nature by chastising the flesh so that the soul might go free; for this purpose he wore for a long time a hair shirt and an iron chain around his body so tightly as to draw blood.

He had someone make him a half-length, tight-fitting coarse undergarment, equipped with 150 sharp brass nails, the points facing the flesh. This was his nightshirt for 16 years.

On simmering summer nights when the heat was almost un- * bearable and he was half-dead from the day's fatigue or from blood-letting, he would fret and squirm sleeplessly from side to side like a worm being pricked with sharp needles. Then there was the annoyance caused by insects. . . .*

The Tension between Spirit and Wholeness

The Blessed Henry Suso, described above, was an extreme example of one who sought the strengthening of spirit at the expense of other aspects of personal life and especially the body, but the direction of his energies was not unusual. The stories of Christian saints are full of ascetic practices, and such practices are by no means limited to Christians. In one form or another they are very widespread. Among American Indians men proved their manhood by showing that they could deny the normal desires of the body and suffer want and pain without flinching. Buddhists meditate on the disgusting character of the body so as to destroy their interest in it. Even you and I, in much milder forms, often deny our bodies the movement they want for the sake of hearing a lecture, reading a book, or completing a conversation. For the sake of decency and social order we deny our bodies the satisfaction of many of their sexual lusts. For ethical reasons we often force our bodies to work when they want to rest.

For the sake of spirit Christians have also undertaken to control emotions. To insure that their actions conform to the highest motivations, feelings of desire, anger, and hostility have been denied and repressed. The self has not only dis-identified with emotions, it has viewed them as alien and dangerous. Again, this is not characteristic only of Christians. The reader of Plato's dialogues is struck by the opposition of the passions to the reason with which the self is identified. But in Christian history, spirit can suppress reason as well, when reason threatens to raise doubts about the beliefs associated with spirit.

In these and other ways the attainment of spirit has been at a frightful cost to other aspects of the psychophysical life. Spirit has brought not peace but a sword into the inner life of Christians. As other aspects of the psychic life—emotion, reason, aesthetic enjoyment, artistic creativity, imagination, and will—have found their champions in modern society, the claims of spirit have become problematic even in the church. In many circles the ideal of spiritual strength has given way to the ideal of harmonious wholeness. For the Christian, too, wholeness can be understood as health and salvation.

Indeed, the question for us today is not whether we are to aim at wholeness, but what *kind* of wholeness we are to achieve. Do we seek the primal wholeness that we lost when we left the womb or outgrew our infancy? Animals, especially wild animals, have a wholeness of body and psyche that human beings lack. Primitive people have a wholeness that disappears with the rise of civilization. Religious myths express this by putting at the beginning of time a unity that has been broken in the course of events. In Christian language we speak of a fall that separated us from the garden of Eden. Is the Christian goal to undo the work of the fall and to return to Eden?

Some of the most persuasive of modern prophets point us in this direction. They point out that wholeness can be attained if we will recognize that we are fundamentally bodily beings and abandon our pretense to be something other than that. In *Life against Death* Norman O. Brown speaks of the resurrection of the body as the release of the body from all the oppression it has suffered at the hands of reason, will, and spirit. He offers a vision of wholeness that is free from tension as the body is freed to be itself and to express itself fully in terms of its own rhythms and needs.*

The Centering of Wholeness in Spirit

The Christian answer to this vision of wholeness is a firm *no*. The kingdom of heaven is not the garden of Eden. There is no returning to primitive innocence. The wholeness of the kingdom will include vastly more than the wholeness of Eden. The wholeness we seek has the simplicity that lies beyond complexity, not the simplicity that precedes it. It is a wholeness centering in spirit. A wholeness centering in spirit is far more difficult to attain than a wholeness centering in body; it must include all the aspects of the psychophysical life, whereas wholeness centering in body or emotions is necessarily attained by destroying reason, will, and spirit or preventing their emergence.

That point needs to be explained. The body with its sexuality is biologically given, and in the animal organism there is also given a unified experience we can call the psyche. Thus human beings like animals are psychophysical organisms. But the psyche of the animal and of the infant does little more than help the body achieve some of its ends. The animal psyche warns the animal of the approach of danger and triggers the appropriate response. The animal is whole, as Norman Brown sees, because in the wild the psyche has no purpose of its own in conflict with the body. The being of the animal centers in the body rather than in the independent purposes of the psyche.

In the human being there is a choice. The psyche is capable of a life of its own, and as the child develops in normal human society, the purposes of the psyche progressively take over leadership from the body. Emotions become more complex and important; there is aesthetic enjoyment; reasoning and willing and imagination appear. But there is no guarantee that the biological development of the human being will bring all of these modes of human functioning into play. Depending on what is prized in a culture, different modes of functioning will be relatively important or unimportant. Choosing between alternatives consciously entertained, for example, has played a far greater role in the orbit of Israel's influence than in other cultures. So we talk easily about the will and freedom of the will, whereas the idea is not clearly expressed in the languages of Asia or even in classical Greek. Today, with different cultural emphases, will is becoming questionable again. In an existence centering in the body there would be no will.

Where the spirit emerges the self is aware of all of these aspects of the psychic life and can make decisions about them as well as about itself. These decisions in much of our Christian past have been to delimit their scope and force upon them what is required for the strengthening of spirit. Thus wholeness has been sacrificed. But as spirit grows strong it need not continue its tyrannous rule. It can give to each aspect of the psychophysical life its appropriate freedom. The full ideal for Christian existence is neither a strong spirit at the expense of wholeness nor wholeness at the expense of spirit, but an inclusive wholeness centering in spirit.

Strengthening the Individual Aspects

This idea of Christian wholeness includes the idea of a strong and healthy body, strong and healthy emotions, a strong and healthy reason, a strong and healthy imagination, and a strong and healthy will, as well as a strong and healthy spirit. No exhaustive list of aspects of psychophysical life ideally included in wholeness is possible, for human existence is inexhaustibly complex. But these examples are sufficient to show that the task of moving toward Christian wholeness is a multifaceted one.

Many aspects of the psychophysical life are already the objects of intensive development in our society. Whereas once the church was extensively involved with physical health and strength, today governments have taken major responsibility. Consideration of diet, exercise, preventive medicine, and therapy is still a part of the church's concern, but when bodily strength and health are viewed in isolation from other aspects of the psychophysical life, the church is not called on to make a major contribution.

The case with emotions is somewhat similar. The awareness of the importance of freeing our emotions from the repression they have suffered so long is now well-established in our dominant culture. Sensitivity groups, various forms of therapy, and many elements in the human potential movement have developed methods of helping people to attain a strong and healthy emotional life. Because the emotional life is so basic to all else in the psychic makeup, and because denial and repression are still important factors in our society, the pastor should share with other leaders in our culture in freeing the emotions and encouraging emotional maturity.

The cultivation of the life of reason was long accepted by the church as a major responsibility, but as in the case of the body, other institutions have now taken over. The church no longer has as a major concern the establishment and operation of schools and universities. It now characteristically looks away from itself for intellectual leadership. This has its problems, but it would be unrealistic to think of the church as reassuming major responsibility for cultivation of the rational faculties.

Still further back in our history, the church also was the chief patron of the imagination as this expressed itself in the arts. That situation is remote from our own. Our need is to encourage Christians to enter more freely into the life of the imagination that is developed chiefly outside our walls. We can open our doors to the contributions of the artist, but we are not equipped to assume responsibility for this dimension of human existence.

The church's role in the strengthening of the will has continued to our own time. No other institution has arisen to take over this responsibility. Indeed the school's role in this respect has declined. However, moves recently have been made in this direction. New forms of therapy have been developed for the purpose of strengthening the will by stressing personal responsibility for what one does. As the church loses its effectiveness in this area, pastors can welcome allies, and they can learn much from these new movements that is applicable to the life of the church and specifically to pastoral counseling.

In the establishment of norms of strength and health of the body, the emotions, the reason, the imagination, and the will, the church has little that is distinctive to say. Specialists in each field are better informed, and the task of the church is to listen and learn. But the church must retain for itself a central concern for a wholistic view and, hence, for how the health and strength of all of these aspects of the psychic life are appropriately related. The church can affirm the methods employed in each area as long as they do not claim too much for the importance of that area against the others. For example, the church supports all those who seek to strengthen the body and make it whole if they do not in the process identify the self with the body or in other ways reduce the possibility of attaining health and strength at other levels. It is in the judgment of the appropriate role of the several aspects in the whole that the distinctive Christian ideal comes into play. Of the many tensions that arise among the several aspects of our existence an example will illustrate how the ideal of wholeness centering in spirit can function.

Emotion, Will, and Spirit

Consider the case—not uncommon a few years ago—of a woman who comes to a pastoral counselor feeling that she is in danger of a nervous breakdown. Marie has had a healthy emotional life with warm ties to family and friends. But she is convinced that the war in Vietnam is morally reprehensible and that the American killing of innocent people is wholly without justification. As a result she has become intensely active in the antiwar movement. Her family and friends do not support her in her new activism and even disapprove of it, so it has been harmful to the personal relationships that are emotionally most important to her. When she acts according to her conscience she pays a high emotional price. When she relaxes and falls back into the emotionally satisfying life she previously enjoyed, her conscience will not let her alone.

How should the counselor deal with Marie? Probably if she is really near a breakdown, the counselor will encourage her to take a rest from her antiwar activity and go camping with her family. But is this a permanent solution? Should she permanently cut out of her life her moral concern to affect public policy? She can most easily achieve some kind of wholeness by this excision. But is this Christian wholeness? Yet if she retains this interest, can she endure the tension between her emotional needs and her ethical commitment?

The counselor has two apparent choices: to strengthen Marie's tendency to identify herself with her emotional needs, and to strengthen her tendency to identify herself with her conscience or will. But either of these moves must be made at the expense of the strength and health of the other aspect of the psychic life. If she identifies herself firmly with her emotional life—and some forms of therapy would encourage this —will or conscience will disappear as a significant factor in her life. If she identifies herself firmly with her moral conviction, she will have to control her natural and healthy emotions.

Pastoral counseling should be able to offer another way. If Marie can realize that she is transcendent of both her emotions and her will, she can appreciate both while denying them absoluteness. She can observe and affirm her strong emotions and her sensitive conscience from a perspective that is neither of them. She can assume responsibility for both and try to bring them toward harmony. She can clarify her aspirations and see the place of both will and emotion in relation to these aspirations. If harmony cannot be attained she can learn to order her life so as to maintain a creative tension between them within the limits that she discovers herself to be capable of sustaining. Thus she can move toward a wholeness centered in spirit.

Reason and Spirit

Although the church can assume but little responsibility for the cultivation of reason as such, it faces an important challenge in another area to which it has not yet addressed itself. This is the question of how reason is employed. This question is dealt with in the university in the sense that the historian and anthropologist show the cultural conditionedness of all thought, the sociologist of knowledge demonstrates how beliefs are shaped by nonrational factors, and the psychologist shows the large role played by rationalization. But the university does not develop methods for freeing reason from these distortions. Indeed, the tendency of education is to encourage the Socratic identification of the self with one's rational activities. The alternative to this that emerges most clearly is expressed in the doctrine of David Hume that reason is and ought to be the slave of the passions.*

Any pastor will recognize the large degree of truth in this doctrine that reason is subordinate to emotion. If one identifies with one's emotionally determined desires, then one employs one's capacity to think as a means of fulfilling these desires. All of us need to examine the extent to which this is true of us personally. For example, we have a strong emotional desire to be seen as good and sensible people both by others and by ourselves. When we do things that are in fact not good and sensible, we often use our reason to think up favorable explanations. Also we go to great lengths to find evidence in support of opinions that we really hold independently of the evidence. In these cases reason is not allowed to carry out its proper work, which is to conform beliefs to available evidence. Unfortunately, no amount of training of the reason insures performance of its proper work. Highly educated people are just as capable of rationalization as are uneducated people. The difference is more in the sophistication with which they marshal evidence to support prejudices than in their genuine openness to reshaping beliefs in light of the evidence. Only as we grow strong in spirit, disidentifying ourselves from both reason and emotion, and then from that perspective examine and correct the way our reason functions, can we in principle overcome the distortion of reason.

The use of reason for its own proper ends is an important contribution to wholeness. Much of the work of counselors is devoted to helping counselees to see the situation as it is and to allow the evidence to shape beliefs and attitudes. Insight therapy in the tradition of psychoanalysis is particularly geared in this direction. Reason is sometimes freed by relieving the emotional pressures that block recognition of the truth, but often its freedom is achieved by encouraging transcendence in the direction of spirit.

The need for reason freed by spirit is a very practical one that is becoming increasingly urgent. Church activities can be brought into line with the real needs of people and the church's own peculiar mission only by a free reason. Without it we cannot move from our present fragmentation toward Christian unity. This can be illustrated in terms of the church's response to the social issues of the day.

The church cannot responsibly be the church without effectively relating itself to social problems. Yet there is no consensus within the churches that would allow corporate action.

To bring up social issues is to be divisive. The attitudes of people are shaped more by their roles and associates outside the church than by their Christian faith. When church leadership tries to take stands in terms of the faith, it is cut off from the support even of devout constituents. Preaching on social issues has only a limited effectiveness and further alienates those who do not share the pastor's view. What is required is joint Christian discussion of the issues to arrive at responsible Christian conclusions. But in the process of discussion, reason is used chiefly to bolster prejudices. In other words, reason functions as the slave of the passions. To call attention to this in the course of the argument only makes people defensive and angry, but if Christians can help each other to become aware of our tendency to rationalize, then in the discussion of particular problems more of us will learn to shape our views by evidence. Progress could be made toward this end in the small-group life of the church.

Spirit and Community

We have discussed how the several aspects of our existence can be individually strengthened so that the whole, centering in spirit, may be healthy. Since more complex issues arise in the relationships among these several aspects, two examples have been considered. The first dealt with the tensions that can arise between emotional needs and ethical concerns. The second focused on how reason can be freed for its own proper work. But all of this discussion has treated the structure of individual existence as if it could be isolated from other people. In fact we exist *in* and *from* and *for* one another. The Christian ideal of wholeness is for personal wholeness in a whole community.

The New Testament teaches us that we are members one of another, jointly belonging to the body of Christ (e.g., Rom. 12:5). There is no personal wholeness apart from intimate participation in one another's lives. Yet Christian history bears witness not only to the difficulty of attaining this ideal but to the tension between it and the strengthening of the individual spirit. The rise of spirit often seems to destroy rather than create wholeness of community.

In tribal existence individuals exist only as members of the tribe. To be separated from that shared life is not to exist at all. Emotions, purposes, and meanings are derived from the tribe and expressed through the members. Elements of tribal existence characterize all of us. What we feel is deeply affected by what those about us feel. Our language is the language of a community. Our beliefs and attitudes are largely determined by what we have been taught and by what is approved in our society. Sociologists confirm what common sense already knows, that for the most part what we think and do is predictable by those who know who our peers and associates are.

The thrust of spiritual existence is to break the power of community over the individual. Insofar as we transcend ourselves, we transcend also the emotions, purposes, and meanings that we derive from others, and we are thus enabled to decide about them. We can constitute ourselves with some freedom in ways that are not produced by the community. In the language of Martin Heidegger, we are capable of *authenticity*.* We become strong individuals, able to stand against the pressure of society, assuming responsibility for what we are and do.

The writings of Heidegger and Sartre depict authentic existence in its isolated individuality and aloneness. They affirm it and exalt it, but they make clear the high price that is paid for it. Individuals share a world with other individuals, but insofar as they are authentic they remain fully external to one another. The presence of others in the shared world is an important factor for each person, but individuals do not contribute to the richness of one another's existence. At a climactic moment in Sartre's play *No Exit*, the protagonist discovers that hell is other people.

The Christian ideal of wholeness in this corporate dimension, like the ideal of wholeness in the intrapsychic dimension, cannot be a return to tribal wholeness. It must be a wholeness attained by mutual participation of authentic or spiritual persons. Something of this sort was witnessed to in the early church, where people freely entered into a community in which their freedom and individuality were reinforced by their shared life. To renew that kind of community in the conditions of our own time and place is now the challenge before us.

One obstacle to the realization of this ideal is a conceptual one. We have come to think that in very truth we *are* separated individuals who can be related to one another only externally. Correlative with the rise of spiritual existence there developed a notion of the self as identical with itself from birth to death. This was understood not as a peculiar characteristic of Christian existence but as a metaphysical fact. The self was thought to be a substance that acted on the world and was acted upon by the world, but as a substance it was necessarily external to all other substances. If this is the reality, then the ideal of mutual participation among selves is unintelligible and illusory. Individual selves, in this view, may do many things for other selves, but they cannot participate in one another.

Only recently have we begun to outgrow this idea of the self. Buddhism has taught us to think in another way. The psyche or soul is nothing but a succession of experiences.* Each of these experiences takes account of all sorts of things and events. The past experiences in a person's life are only one portion of this total world. Similarly, the momentary experience does not contribute only to those future events which will constitute that person's life. It contributes the experiences of others as well.

If this is true, then the way that others participate in us and we in them is not fundamentally different from the way our past participates in our present or our present in our future. Love is not simply an external act upon others but an empathetic acceptance of others and a giving of ourselves to participate in the lives of others. The ideal of being united to one another in a single body is not illusory. It only fails to be lived out to a sufficient degree to overcome our conceptual reasons for disbelief. If we can reappropriate it in our thought and imagination, the ideal can gain a power that will suggest to us modes of implementation.

A mutually participating community of self-transcending selves will be very different from a tribal community. The appropriation from others will not be mere conformation to dominant emotions, attitudes, and opinions. It will instead be selective integration of what is most original and creative in the potential contribution of these others. Even where feelings are empathetically shared, the sharing will be freely chosen. In the process the self-transcendence of spirit will be strengthened.

Although this overcoming of individual isolation in favor of inclusion of the others has its primary relevance in the reconception of community, it is also important for the shaping of other aspects of our sensibility. Global consciousness will not take adequate root in us until we sense the depths of our actual unity with all other people and even with the whole biosphere. Only as we feel that the suffering of other persons and the destruction of other species diminishes us will we be able to bring our actions into line with what is required by our self-transcending spirit. The feeling and sensibility needed is already present within us. What is now called for is the freedom to recognize in these intuitions of unity the metaphysical truth rather than childish sentimentality. The church can encourage their strengthening and clarification rather than exhort us to dismiss them in the name of realism.

Marriage

The form of community that comes most to the fore in counseling is marriage. Marriage counseling must reflect the pastor's views with respect to what marriage should be, and the new self-consciousness of women has made our present institution problematic. This chapter will conclude with comments on what Christian marriage has been and should become in light of the ideal of wholeness in community.

Some marital problems illustrate the tension that prevails between the ideal of Christian wholeness and the ideal of participatory community. Women have brought to the focus of our consciousness our previously dim awareness that in Christendom, as in many other cultures, women have been denied full participation in the ideals of human wholeness held before men. Throughout the centuries down to our own time the social pressure exerted on males to become strong self-transcending individuals has not been exerted to an equal degree upon women. In fact, through most of this period women have been excluded from full participation in educational and religious institutions. Like slaves they were often intentionally kept in a childlike state, or one in which the transcendence of the self over the bodily and emotional life was minimized. Even in recent times, as the rigid barriers crumbled, social expectations continued to push women in the same direction, and marriage, the most basic of social institutions, shared in exerting this pressure.

A major reason for this pattern was the sexual needs and attitudes of the male. The male valued psyche, and especially spirit above body, and this led to a suppression of the body for the sake of spirit. For the most part this did not mean the abandonment of sexual activity, but the provision of the opportunity for sexual expression was a concession to weakness. If one could engage in sex without moderating one's self-transcending selfhood then there would be little harm, but in fact the full enjoyment of sexuality required an abandonment of inhibiting controls over the body. It required instead a centering of existence in the body. This was experienced as degrading. From the perspective of spirit the enjoyment felt along with this degradation could only elicit disgust. But the problem was ameliorated insofar as the sexual partner was felt to belong to the level to which the male was descending. To abandon oneself to bodiliness in the presence of one with whom one had relations at the level of reason and spirit would be more difficult and more revolting than to become a body in the company of another body. Hence the male desired that his sexual companion be as purely bodily as possible. It was then even possible to feel that the blame for the degradation lay upon the one who brought the male to a level with herself.

As long as marriage operated in this context it did not make much difference, from the point of view of women's liberation, whether the woman was free to choose her mate or not. Once the mate was chosen, the patterns of social expectation set by the supposed differences between the sexes predetermined what her role would be. Although greatly modified in recent times, a socially enforced hierarchy has characterized marriage down to our own day.

From the point of view of the Christian ideal all people should be encouraged as far toward spiritual existence as they will go. A social arrangement that militates against the full spiritualization of any group in the society is anti-Christian. The religious tendency to sanction the status quo, even the institution of marriage, when it operates to inhibit the full liberation of spiritualization of women, must be opposed.

One experiment in new patterns is a contractual arrangement. Marriage is entered into conditionally. Each partner agrees to meet certain conditions and each shares equally in determining what these conditions are. In this way social definitions of roles are broken, and the marriage represents the coming together of two equals for purposes jointly agreed upon.

If the Christian's only concern were the individual strength of each person, contractual marriage could be wholeheartedly approved. But the Christian is equally concerned for community. The Christian ideal is that each person be supported by a rich participation in the lives of others. The participation should be free and equal, but it can occur only where there is unconditional commitment.   Some elements of mutual participation were nurtured in traditional marriage, in spite of the inequality of roles.   As relative equality has been approached some marriages have moved toward a rich level of personal communion and mutual participation between wife and husband.   Contractual marriage breaks those relations.

We are in one of the frequently encountered situations where the full attainment of the ideal is rarely possible; we must often choose between truncated approaches.   The choice may be between a contractual arrangement in which the woman has opportunity for personal liberation and a participatory marriage in which social roles still introduce elements of restriction, especially upon the woman.   But the ideal is clear.   Even for the sake of liberation both partners need the support of a participatory community, and the community with the spouse is ideally the best opportunity.   For genuine participation to occur, those who participate must do so as fully developed individuals with their autonomous strength.

There is a particular challenge to Christian teaching in the demands made by women and by others seeking liberation. The attitude of demanding one's rights and laying down conditions for service seems diametrically opposed to the New Testament teaching about sacrifice as the way of life.   Pastors often recognize that calling on counselees to sacrifice is inappropriate, but there is less clarity as to how to relate this recognition to continuing commitment to the Christian way. The discussion here may throw some light on this vexing problem.

The New Testament does not lay down a new set of laws to replace the old.   When it is read in that light it becomes the most repressive law ever promulgated, capable only of producing guilt and despair.   The New Testament does describe the new life that ideally follows from one's transformation into Christian existence.   That is a life that is free from the law. But Christians have not always understood this distinction.

Accordingly, they have tried to formulate ethical principles which they have held before people as normative. They have held these principles before people, whether or not people had attained existence in the spirit. The results have been mixed. Sometimes the high demands of "Christian ethics" have elicited life-transforming aspirations and have led toward Christian existence. Sometimes these demands have been rejected with destructive feelings of guilt. Sometimes people try but fail and are led to despair. Sometimes the ideals are appropriated without the spiritual existence to which this style of life is suited.

In our century it has often been pointed out that while white males, who have had the greatest opportunities for spiritualization, give only lip service to the ideal of sacrificial service, they have inculcated it successfully in their women and in minority groups who have not had equal opportunity to develop fully individualized personal strength. Acceptance of the ideal as a moral principle has then inhibited the move toward personal strength. What has been sacrificed is not the self-transcending spiritual self, for that has not been attained. What is sacrificed instead is the possibility of *becoming* a spiritual self.

When this is realized by the victims of the self-sacrifice, the angry reaction is often directed at Christianity and its ideals. It is felt that Christian teaching misdirects energies and establishes false goals. Since this has been the actual experience of millions of people, the charge must be taken seriously. But if the position presented here is correct, the fault lies not in the New Testament account of Christian existence but in its misuse as law. Christians are called to help their neighbors grow to the fullness of Christian existence. As that fullness is attained, the New Testament account of how it is expressed in the mutuality of Christian community becomes relevant. Awareness of this possibility for life may serve to heighten aspirations and to strengthen incipient spirit. But there are many ways toward Christian existence, and for many people the self-assertion of the responsible self against unreasonable and inappropriate demands is a major step toward that existence. As long as this is recognized as what is needed *now*, and is not turned into an ultimate ideal of existence, the Christian can and should call for self-assertion of all those who need liberation from unreasonable demands and expectations. In some measure that is all of us.

4. God and Pastoral Care

When Wayne E. Oates asks the question, "What makes counseling pastoral?" his primary answers introduce God. He speaks of "the God-in-relation-to-persons consciousness" and of God as differentiating the pastoral counselor's conception of reality from that of other counselors.* Oates is right. In chapters 2 and 3 I have proposed a distinctive way to think of Christian existence that can guide pastoral care and counseling, but unless this is seen in relation to God, its truly Christian character will not appear. The church is bound up with belief in divine reality, and so is the role of the pastor. But in our secular age the sense of divinity has become obscure. The ideas of God brought by counselees are more likely to be part of their problem than a contribution to health and growth, and pastoral counselors are often too insecure in their own sense of the divine to bring it into effective and realistic relation to the counseling process.

If pastors now want to differentiate their counseling in this way, they must ask the central theological question, What is God? In seeking an answer to this question they have every right to expect help from professional theologians. Unfortunately, they turn to theology at a time of confusion. Yet emerging out of the confusion of the last few years one may dare to discern a new consensus, not about a *concept* of God, but about where God is to be found in our reality. This chapter offers an entry for ministers into this emerging consensus, and discusses how it can give direction to their pastoral care.

God as No-Thing .

To the question, What is God? the first answer is, "Nothing." That answer can have a number of meanings.

Some people may mean that the question is unimportant, and often we should respect their feelings. Some seem satisfied to deal with individual things and people and institutions on an ad hoc or purely conventional basis. Perhaps they do not experience the wonder about ordinary things which gives rise to science and philosophy. What they themselves are made of, where they come from, or where they are going are likewise not questions for them. But for many people questions of this sort do arise. Most people want to understand their world, and the quest for understanding makes the question about God important.

The answer "Nothing" may also be a profound response to questions that have been asked with keenest intensity and penetration. It is an answer that is common to the mystics. There is, they teach us, no *thing* that surrounds, unifies, underlies, or controls the particular things we find about us. That means that all our images and ideas fail us when we try to think our way past these particulars; for all these images and ideas are of things. There is no Supreme Being alongside other beings. There is no unifying substance underlying all the events of the world. But mystics teach us that unity with this inconceivable and unspeakable No-Thing is blessedness.

Mysticism has an honored place in Christian tradition. The mystic insistence on the No-Thingness of God rightly checks the tendency to identify our ideas and images of the divine with the divine itself. We have historically invested so much in these ideas and images that when they have been proved false or inappropriate—and this is the fate of all ideas and images—we have often despaired. We have supposed that we have discovered the nonexistence of the divine thing. We should have used the occasion to relearn the lesson that the divine is No-Thing.

God as Transcendent: The Creator

Nevertheless the Christian community cannot live by mysticism alone. In stressing that God is No-Thing, mystics so contrast God with all particular things, and with all that we can think or imagine, that, whether they intend to do so or not, they discourage the continuing task of thinking about particulars, their purposes and their deeper meanings. Entrenched in Christian tradition is the view that the divine is Creator of all the particular things. That makes these particulars important; it makes the study of the particulars important; and as a result we have developed history and science to a degree that more mystically inclined cultures have not. It also makes theology important as the discipline that tries to work out the best ideas and images it can about the unthinkable and unimaginable divine Creator. In spite of all the dangers entailed, the Christian effort to get rightly related to God involves a discussion of ideas and images, an attempt to distinguish the more accurate and appropriate from the more misleading.

But the traditional view of God as Creator has come into difficulty. It places the Creator outside the creatures. Even though Christian theology has known that this outsideness is not spatial, the images that have dominated the liturgy and rhetoric of the church have been spatial. As those images have clashed more sharply with the dominant images of modern thought, they have lost their power.

. Furthermore, we have had difficulty with the idea of the Creator itself. It is hard to separate it entirely from some note of temporal priority. But we no longer think of our world as having a beginning in time. Or if we do, that beginning was so long ago, and what began then is so different from the world we know, that the question of the ultimate origin is not very important for us. Our interest attaches to how our present world has developed from that ancient explosion or cloud of gases. What is important to us is not the cause of the "big bang" that may have occurred ten to fifteen billion years ago, but the cause of life, health, growth, and community today and tomorrow. Our thought must shift from a once-for-all creation to a continuous creative activity. But how can we conceive of that activity? Is it an action upon things from without? Do things as we know them from moment to moment give evidence of such an external action upon them? It seems that they do not. Thus the externality that is bound up in the sense of the Creator does not fit with the modern view that there is no externality, either spatial or temporal, to that whole community of particular things that is the world. The modern Western experience of "the death of God" was in part a loss of the sense of an external Creator. Once again we have been forced to recognize that there is no thing, in Bishop Robinson's words, "up there" or "out there."*

God as Incarnate: Directivity

If there is no thing which is the Creator above or beyond the universe, how are we to think of the creative and the divine? The answer is that God must be found in the world. But where? What factor in the ongoing actuality of the world speaks of divinity?

The easiest analysis of things is their analysis into form and into matter. We can readily distinguish the shape of a table from the wood of which it is made. The wood in its turn can be seen to have a paticular form, and its matter can be analyzed chemically until we come to what Aristotle called *prime matter* and what we today are more likely to call *energy* or *being*. Both philosophy and science have focused on this kind of distinction and its resulting analysis, and sometimes the divine has been associated either with the forms of things or with their matter.

However, from ancient times another aspect of things has sometimes been recognized. It is more mysterious and elusive than form or matter. It is not manifest in inorganic things such as rocks and sand, although incipiently it may be present in the particles that make these up. But in living things and in human experience it is clearly important. This factor is an orientation toward the future, an aim, a directionality, a goal-directedness. We will call it *directivity*.

In our discussion of Chester Carter and of Brent and Marge we spoke of aspiration as wanting to be what one is not. In their cases this aspiration was not strong, but even in them, unrealized possibilities for their existence exercised some effective influence. What was for them *not-yet* in some measure called or claimed them and introduced an urge toward self-transcendence or spirit. This is what we are now calling directivity.

Chester, Brent, and Marge may not have been aware of this directivity. Pastors Jones and Scott hardly noticed it themselves. But pastors can attend to it and encourage it. They can even bring it to the attention of those whom they counsel. As we become more aware of its presence, its effectiveness increases.

The Greeks sensed this feature of things. Aristotle spoke of the "final cause" of things alongside the formal, material, and efficient causes.* In the modern world, as forms became abstractions and matter became energy and dynamic Being, directivity, when acknowledged, was attributed to matter instead of to its final cause. In Karl Marx's dialectical materialism, matter drives toward the classless society.† Paul Tillich attributes to Being-Itself, which is the "ground" of being energizing all beings, an urge toward the overcoming of brokenness and the preservation of values.‡

It is striking that both for the Greeks and for the moderns directivity is associated with the divine. For Aristotle, the final cause of all motion or change is God. For Marxists, despite disclaimers, an aura of divinity attaches to the dialectical process. For Tillich, Being-Itself *is* God. This association of directivity with God is still clearer in the Bible. Yahweh has purposes for the world, and from the divine purposes persons derive theirs. Furthermore, directivity is far more central to biblical thought than to that of either Greeks or moderns. Too often this has been obscured by efforts to explain Christian faith in terms of Greek philosophy or modern science.

Recently, however, there has been an explosion of awareness that the directivity in things, and especially in human existence, cannot be assimilated to either form or matter. William James taught us to think of an open universe in which our acts shape the future.* Existentialists describe human existence in terms of decisions in light of the open future for which we are responsible. Ernst Bloch has showed that human decision is made in relation to unrealized possibilities that transcend the past, and he spoke of these, as they are relevant to us, as *das Novum*, "the new."† Teilhard de Chardin gave us a vision of the whole universe moving toward a radically new future.‡ Alfred North Whitehead has provided a rich account of how the aim that is present in all things derived from God.§ Christian theologians have recognized that what is coming to expression here is what has all along been most closely related to the Christian experience of the divine. The divine No-Thing opens up the future to us and calls us to realize appropriate new possibilities. God is thus the one who frees us to transform the past rather than merely repeat it. Once directivity toward the new future is brought clearly to consciousness, Christians can recognize that it is central to their sensibility of what is divine and what orders their world. To be rightly related to God is to be rightly related to this directivity at the heart of things.

Directivity as a thrust toward the future is not an aspect or factor present in things, as are form and matter. Form and matter can be discerned in things without reference to the future. But directivity is aimed toward the future, toward unrealized possibilities, that is, toward *what-is-not-yet*. On the other hand, these unrealized possibilities must truly function in the present if there is to be directivity at all. They must be present as effective lures to new realization and action. Thus

what-is-not-yet is always transcendent of *what-is*, but it produces directivity in *what-is* only as it becomes immanent.
Directivity is always a matter of the transcendent becoming
immanent, that is, of the incarnation of the transcendent.

This means that when we think of God as directivity we
think of incarnation. God transcends the world as the giver
of all new possibility. It is because of God that *what-is-not-
yet* can come into being. It is by becoming present or incarnate as their directivity that God renders the appropriate *what-
is-not-yet* effective as an aim or lure, energizing and directing
the activity of each thing and person. In this way God, as the
source of unrealized possibility, inexhaustibly transcends the
world, but it is precisely *as* transcendent that God is immanent
in the directivity that moves in and through all living things.
Thus God as Creator is not only transcendent but also fully
and radically incarnate.

The Discernment of God

If the directivity that is in things, and especially in people, is
the incarnate presence of God in them, then we all have to do
with God all the time. That might seem to make the business
of being rightly related to God all too easy. We might suppose that things would go along as God wanted, whether we
think about him or not, and that the process is more or less
automatic; much Christian talk about the sovereignty of God
has encouraged that supposition, intentionally or not. But
Christian experience and theology over the years have pointed
to human responsibility as much as to divine grace.

The directivity in things is due to God. If there were no yet
unrealized possibilities that we could experience as real op-
tions there would be no openness, no space, within which we
could exercise responsibility. But because the *not-yet* is incarnate in *what-is*—that is, because we experience possibilities
that we *can* realize, but don't have to—there is, on our part,
decision. God gives us freedom: not a general capacity built
into human nature, but a specific freedom in each new situa-

tion. To exercise that freedom is to choose for the possibility we receive from God, the possibility that makes us free. Not to choose that possibility is to surrender to bondage. To use the freedom we receive is to become open to still new possibilities. Our freedom increases as God becomes more fully immanent in us. To refuse the gift of freedom is to shut God out. The existentialists are right about the importance of decision.

But if being rightly related to God is just to be deciding all the time, that seems to make it a pretty simple, if a rather strenuous, affair. Yes and no! The Christian gospel is a very simple matter, and so is the faith in which it is appropriated. But it is also a straight and narrow way that is to be found in the midst of all sorts of possible distortions. To be rightly related to the divine is quite simply to trust God; but truly to *trust*, and to put trust truly in *God*, is a perfection that is all too easy to miss.

One great need is discernment. Earlier in this chapter it was shown that the philosophical tradition, while bearing witness indirectly to the reality of the directivity in things, has failed to discern it clearly. It has focused on the analysis of *what-is*. For the thinker, *what-is-not-yet* is not there to be analyzed, and the strange presence of *what-is-not-yet* in *what-is* does not conform to the categories that work so well, otherwise, for understanding *what-is*. We are all to some extent philosophers, or at least we all have our attention directed through our language to the aspects of the world that philosophers have seen. It is a special task of the church, the heir and custodian of the Bible, to call our attention to the directivity in things that has almost eluded other traditions.

Even when our attention is turned to this directivity and we recognize that it is the divine presence in the world, the task of discernment has just begun. Where is it heading? To what is it directing us? The difficulty is that we never find the directivity by itself. It is always a factor in experiences that are crowded with other elements—insistent bodily cravings and emotional needs. The several aspects of experience don't come clearly labeled. The history of Christianity is replete with people who have named their own desires the will of God. If there is self-deception involved, it is not always conscious. One task of spiritual growth is to learn to discern the divine presence in the midst of the chaotic crosscurrents of feeling, thought, and imagination that make up our experience.

There are some general remarks of the divine directivity in things that can provide parameters for this discernment. The divine presence is the life of the world. Quite literally, it is this directivity in things that constitutes all life. Where there is no aim to become something new, where *what-is-not-yet* does not function as a lure, things can only repeat the past, and the repetition is never perfect. The result is always necessarily what physicists call *entropy*. But where conditions allow for novelty, and where novelty prevails, there is life. Life is always a transcendence and transformation of given conditions, a thrust toward a future. Christians have recognized that the same is true on a greater scale for human existence. Beyond biological life are human life, personal life, and spiritual life. The work of God within us is to quicken us, to give us life—new life, and more abundant life. Today we talk of the movement of human life toward its own enhancement and intensification as personal growth. In chapters 2 and 3 I have offered a picture of personal wholeness centered in spirit and in the context of community to indicate the direction in which Christians discern this growth. It is always God who is the call to growth and the giver of growth. The growth occurs through the divine incarnation. The more we understand about life and growth, the better we can discern God at work within us and among us.

Growth is never the simple addition of something new to what is already present. If it were, it would not be resisted so strongly. Instead, to add the new is to change the old. That does not mean that the old is simply wiped out or cast aside.

That would not be growth but mere change. It does mean that the old is transformed in the renewing of our minds. It must receive, quite literally, a new form. Because we identify ourselves with *what-is*, with what we have achieved, with what we already are, the opportunity for growth is always also a threat. We can let the *not-yet* transform us only by letting go of what we are. And we must let go of what we are without knowing in advance what we will become. Growth is not the working out of a pattern that we have planned for ourselves. It does not follow lines that we can predetermine, for it involves the emergence of ways of thinking and feeling that are new. Our plans cannot go beyond the elements that are already present in experience. To allow growth to take place is always a risk. This is why trust is so important. We cannot grow without surrendering the effort to control the future. But to surrender this effort is not to become passive, just to let the powerful forces of the world buffet us about. That would be the opposite of trust in God. That would be to let the world determine everything. That is the way of death. Christian existence is a life of constant decision in the context of the gift of God's presence; it is the continual choosing of life.

God and Counseling

When we think of our life with God in this way, the commitment to God and the sense of God's effective presence moves to the heart of the counseling situation. Counseling for growth is direct service of God. The counselor is observing God's working in the counselee, helping to remove some of the barriers to that working, and encouraging the tentative steps toward openness to life, and therefore to God, that have brought the counselee to seek help from a fellow human being. Pastors above all will know that they are at most midwives of God's grace. They do not cause the growth. It is not for them to predetermine where the growth will lead. They can counsel rightly only if they trust God.

The clear recognition that pastoral counseling is an expression of trust in God helps to prevent the counselors' agenda from getting in the way. Pastors have their own needs, for self-esteem, for example, and there is nothing to insure that these will be set aside during the counseling session. But the greatest need of pastors is to grow. If the fundamental understanding of what is occurring in the counseling session is that God is being trusted, then the pastors' spirit of trust opens them to growth as well. Counseling cannot be of the one who needs to grow by the one who has arrived. It can only be of one growing person by another. Pastors must let themselves be transformed if they are to help open the counselees to transformation as well.

Pastors who recognize that what is making for growth in the counseling situation is God's incarnate presence may find that there are occasions for calling the attention of counselees to this fact. Clearly the introduction of this language is not required for growth to occur, and in many cases the connotations may be such that it would do more harm than good. But to name that which is occurring through the counseling as God, or Christ, or the Holy Spirit, or grace, can also facilitate the process. Trust can be strengthened when it has a clearer focus. A name can give that focus; and for the person whose experience with Christian language has been healthy, the name of Christ encourages trust. To use that name can also tie in the experience in the counseling sessions with the rest of the counselees' Christian experience and life in the church, to the benefit of both. It can do this best if there are groups in the church that are working together to strengthen one another in the discernment of the working of the divine and in the appropriate alignment of their lives.

Discernment Groups

Groups organized to increase responsiveness to God need a clear idea of what they are trying to do. Such groups are in continuity with forms of spirituality that have operated in the church throughout the centuries, but they also embody differences from many forms of traditional spirituality, reflecting the differences between traditional ideas and the way God was presented in this chapter.

Some spirituality has been mystical. In its extreme form, mystical spirituality turns attention away from all particulars and withdraws energy from involvement in the world. The spirituality now required attends to the particularity of the directivity in each moment.

Some spirituality has subordinated the self to the Creator. When the Creator is supposed to be all powerful, so that whatever happens expresses his will, the appropriate spirituality is resignation to what happens, however cruel it appears to be. The spirituality now required is one of shaping an open future in accordance with relevant possibilities given by God.

Some spirituality has been geared to ascertaining and obeying the divine will. When God is thought to be radically transcendent, that will must be revealed from without. Accordingly, one must decide where that revelation occurs and then believe and obey it whether the ideas and commandments make sense or not. The spirituality now required attends not so much to commandments given once for all as to opportunities that are fresh in every moment.

Some spirituality has been oriented to strengthening oneself as an ethical being. When God is supposed to have given us reason and conscience and freedom of the will, it seems supremely important that we describe moral principles correctly and apply them rightly. The spirituality now required checks and supplements rational calculation of duty by immediate sensitivity to the divine directivity.

Some spirituality, in its dissatisfaction with moral casuistry as a means for guiding life, has sought special guidance through new revelations or other ecstatic experiences. The spirituality now required attends to an ordinary factor in ordinary experience in order to bring it into extraordinary focus and effectiveness. It does not exclude the possibility that the presence of God will be clarified and dramatized in extra-ordinary experiences.

But some spirituality already has well-developed approaches and attitudes appropriate to the understanding of God as incarnate in directivity. The Jesuits have ways of discerning the Spirit. The Quakers have means of heightening sensitivity to the inner light. To move forward to new patterns of spirituality in the church will be gratefully to learn from the past.

Chapters 2 and 3 described a Christian understanding of the direction in which the divine activity draws us. From such an understanding we can draw many conclusions to guide our lives and our corporate practice in the church. The church can live in this way. But this is not spiritual discernment. That discernment is of God's activity directly in the particular instance and is not deduced by reason from general principles.

The conscious cultivation of such mature spirituality is not for all. The emphasis here is on discerning God's offer and call forward in every situation. This is contrasted with applying an objectively given knowledge of God to the situation. But if we try in a vacuum to discern what God is doing within us, there is little chance of success. We will not know where to look or how to discriminate. All sorts of impulses and images suggested by our unconscious life will be confused with the divine directivity. We will lack patience and judgment. Judgment is nourished through rich experience with other Christians and with the Scriptures. An understanding of psychology, and especially of the tricks that the mind plays on one, is needed. Academic knowledge of such matters will not suffice, for it can only be translated into rules. Further, we learn in the Bible that God calls us to work for justice and liberation, so that those whose Christian experience has been confined to working with family and friends will not have the horizons of sensitivity for reliable discernment. There is no substitute for broad experience in the attainment of wisdom.

This is not to say that Christians should delay cultivation of sensitivity to the working of God until they have reached years of exalted wisdom. But the movement of the Christian life is from guidance by established authorities toward full autonomy of personal judgment. The church is a community in which that process should take place. Children learn from adults. Adults participate in many activities that broaden their horizons and heighten their sensitivity to the divine directivity. Increasingly they sense how they are being borne forward by a power they do not control. They recognize that their acts of decision are made in the context of a gift. They become more sensitive to the ever-changing content of the gift, and their decisions are more fully expressive of that content. Trust in God is the essence of all Christian life. But the conscious and focused cultivation of the discernment of the spirit belongs rather later than earlier. Conscious discernment grows out of unconscious responsiveness developed in the living of Christian life, guided by the community and its Scriptures.

5. Renewing the Language

For pastoral counseling to come of age it was necessary for it to turn away from the images and rhetoric of traditional piety. Those images and that rhetoric had once spoken of the deepest and most encompassing aspects of the experience of Christians, but they had been gradually reduced to a special ecclesiastical language whose relevance, if there was any, was limited to a single dimension of life. The images and rhetoric of the human sciences and especially of psychology were the real language about the real needs and problems of life. Pastors necessarily turned to psychology to help them help people.

But as in so many forms of progress, something was lost. Features of experience that had once been highlighted and reinforced by Christian language were obscured by psychological language. The goals of the psychological schools differed subtly from one another and from the historic goals of Christianity. To borrow language and methodology from these schools was also to introduce their aims and purposes into the activity of counseling. A tension developed between counseling and preaching. To adjust the purposes of preaching to those of counseling only made the continuity of the church with its Christian past still more obscure. The interpretation of the church in simply sociopsychological terms became increasingly plausible. It seemed to be an institution more or less sensitive to the best thought of its time but with no message of its own. As Christian the church has to deal with the real needs of real people. In order to do so, it seemed, the church had to give up all that made it distinctively Christian.

A Secular Christian Rhetoric

The preceding chapters offered one kind of response to this situation. They made little use of traditional theological language, and in that sense they shared in the post-Christian situation of the church. But they attempted to state in post-Christian language what the impact of Jesus Christ has been and now can be in the world through the church. In that sense they offered an understanding of the proper purposes of the church in a form that can enter into the contemporary arena of discussion as that arena is shaped by the human sciences and philosophical reflection. Much recent theology has been of this sort.

Still this is not a satisfactory solution. The language of faith conveys meanings that are missed even in the best translations. The church lives by its ever-renewed encounter with its sources, and it cannot fully appropriate those sources apart from their language. The gap in most liberal churches between the language of the Scriptures and hymns and the language used in the sermons (to say nothing of the counseling sessions) is not a mark of health. If the church is to regain health it must recover the ability to use historic Christian imagery and rhetoric with power and authenticity.

Our Language and Biblical Language

When the need to reestablish contact with this language is recognized, the first response is to find equivalents in contemporary idiom. Words like *alienation, defensiveness*, and *closedness* have meaning to us as modern people, whereas *sin* does not. Perhaps then we can decide that the meaning of *sin* in the Bible is the same as what is meant by *alienation* or *defensiveness* or *closedness* today. With such an understanding we can once again use the word *sin*.

There is both value and danger in this approach. It does help the modern person to find meaning in the reading of the

Bible, and it might prove an avenue for reintroducing the word *sin* into our vocabulary. But to the extent that the word *sin* is understood to have just the meaning of these more acceptable words, the value of using it is reduced. The word *sin* in the Bible has its own integrity of meaning interconnected with the meanings of other biblical words. For example, it carried the note of personal and corporate responsibility without reducing the context to a moral one. It lifted to consciousness, in the community in which it was used, dimensions of experience that are not the same as those elicited by our modern words. Thus it contributed to a world of meaning that is different from the dominant ones of our time. To translate the words of that different world into our language makes them meaningful to us, but it does so by denying them their own meanings.

We have here a dilemma. The church needs to establish a living relationship to the language of the Bible. But the present world of meaning is different from the world of meaning that the biblical language expresses. We cannot simply go back to that earlier world, and to the extent that the church tries to do so it is not faithful to its own genius. On the other hand, to translate the biblical language into our language is to falsify it and rob it of its own power. If we allow the Bible to say to us only what we already know and can say more clearly in our own way, then we can do without the Bible, and we should abandon all pretense that we believe in its authority.

Albert Schweitzer dealt movingly with this problem at the beginning of the century. In his famous book *The Quest of the Historical Jesus* he concluded that Jesus was, by our standards, an apocalyptic fanatic and a world-denier.* Schweitzer did not, for this reason, exhort us to change our standards to conform to Jesus. We would be wrong to surrender either our belief that the world will not end as Jesus expected or our world-affirming stance. That means that we cannot translate Jesus' message into our language-world. If we are honest, we will recognize it as utterly strange to us.

But Schweitzer did not think that Jesus was unimportant to

us. We need to encounter him, that is, to meet him in all his strangeness as a challenge to what we take so easily for granted. We need to work out our own affirmation of the world in the teeth of his powerful and passionate denial.

New Testament scholars often share with Schweitzer this sense of the strangeness of the New Testament world, on the one hand, and the sense of the importance to us of encountering it in its integrity, on the other. In this way it is allowed to challenge us and to confront us with possibilities for our existence to which we would otherwise be blind. Karl Barth spoke of "the strange new world within the Bible."* And Rudolph Bultmann understood the deepest purpose of all study of history to be bringing to bear upon us different ways of understanding existence, so that we are enabled and compelled to choose among them.†

Some of the best preaching of modern times has reflected this sense of the tension between the biblical world and ours. But it is harder to make use of this style in counseling. There the world of the counselee must be taken as the basic context in which healing and growth are to take place. The counselor may help to expand that world through new insights, but to confront it with the biblical world is likely to be counterproductive.

Can biblical language be used authentically without this sharp over-againstness? I believe that it can be. Hans-Georg Gadamer has written of the merging of the horizons of the past and the present.‡ By expanding our own modes of thought in dialogue with the biblical world of thought, the meaning of the latter, in its own integrity, can become a part of an enlarged meaning-world for us. If so, the introduction of biblical language into our world would not draw us back into an archaic world but would draw us forward into a new one. The new world would grow out of the present world but would be able to absorb some of the past meanings that the contemporary world has lost.

Events since Schweitzer wrote have made this seem more

hopeful with respect to Jesus.   On the one hand, contemporary scholarship draws quite a different picture of Jesus.
Apocalyptic expectation, if present to him, was not all-deter-
minative.   His world-denial, if that is a useful way of seeing
him, was far from unqualified.   On the other hand, we are less
opposed to apocalyptic and world-denying modes of thought
than were our grandparents at the beginning of this century.
Talk of the end of history seems far from meaningless in light
of the nuclear arsenal and the environmental crisis.   More
radically world-denying modes of thought than that of Jesus
have taken hold of the contemporary imagination, some
stemming from the East and others evolving out of the Western experience.   In some respects we find ourselves closer to
Jesus than to the more recent historical milieu to which
Schweitzer gave expression.

This suggests that the time may have come for us to bring
our language-world and that of the Bible together, while al-
lowing the biblical language to retain its own meaning.   The
risks of such an attempt are considerable.   We may end up
losing the cutting edge of both biblical and modern thought.
But the potential gains are great.   We could look forward to a
church that has something to say that is distinctive without
being archaic, that illumines secular experience while affirming the rich insights to which that experience has given rise.
Pastoral counselors could experience their counseling not simply as in continuity with Christianity in its ultimate purposes
but as informed by the Christian heritage in both form and
substance.

But if this is to happen, it must grow out of the living
experience of Christian people who are fully immersed in the
modern world.   They must find that the authentic use of biblical language illumines their experience and brings to consciousness aspects of that experience that have been neglected
or obscured by modern conceptualities.   It must become natural to think partly in biblical language, not only in hothouses
of piety or in the interpretation of very special experiences,

but in the understanding of ordinary life. If this occurs, and only when it occurs, will it become proper and natural to employ such language in pastoral counseling.

In the remainder of this chapter I want to suggest how the renewed use of a few elements of biblical language might look. Rather than describe abstractly what I am envisioning, I offer a story of the interaction of a laywoman and her pastor, in which a few traditional words and phrases become meaningful and illuminating for them. The understanding of God as Christ and as grace reflects the ideas developed above in chapter 4.

Alice Bristol and Pastor Carlstone

Alice Bristol called to ask her pastor if she could come over to talk with him. He agreed. She had not sought counseling since her decision to drop out of the Master of Christian Education program at the seminary after one year, but today she was seething with anger, and her usual means of dealing with it were not working. She was particularly bothered because the cause of the anger was so trivial. Bill, her husband, had dropped several sections of the newspaper on the floor as he hurried to work. The anger came on her when, shortly after he had kissed her goodbye, she had stooped to pick them up.

Of course, Alice knew that her anger was caused by the fact that Bill took for granted that it was her place to straighten things up. After all, he brought home the bacon, and there was nothing Alice had to do but look after the house and one child. And although she was an influential leader in both church and community, she *could* arrange her schedule to pick up things Bill dropped. Bill was a loving and generous husband, and Alice knew she was lucky. She was ready to confess her fault.

Even so, she looked forward to telling Pastor Carlstone about some of the incidents that irritated her so. He would understand how annoying it was to be taken for granted, and he might go deeper into her past experience to find the sources for the intensity of her irritation.   She could tell him some stories of how her father, much more unreasonably than Bill, had taken her services for granted in her adolescence after her mother died.   Maybe she was displacing hostility toward her father onto her husband.   That would be interesting to discuss.

But the interview did not go like that.   Pastor Carlstone listened as she told of her anger and noted how disproportionate it was to the cause, but he did not pick up his cue to inquire about the deeper causes.   He simply asked, "Why do you let him get away with it?"   She began explaining what a good husband he was and how she had the time to straighten up the house.   He interrupted her, "If it makes you so angry, why don't you tell him to stop doing things like that?"

She was nonplussed.   She wanted to say, "But Pastor, aren't we called as Christians to loving sacrifice?   Isn't this a very small cross for me to bear?"   But that sounded awfully pious.   She left abruptly.

The pastor's question made Alice realize that the reason she could not correct her husband was her image of herself as a good Christian.   Her self-approval was bound up with this image.   In short, she saw that it was her concern to be righteous that was getting in her way.   At that point there flashed into her mind a phrase she had heard in seminary: *justification by faith*.   Why, of course!   That was the Christian answer— or at least the Protestant answer.   But for the first time in her life she began to wonder what it meant.   That shocked her. She was so competent in such matters.   She knew how to think.   And she had even read books that discussed justification by faith.   She had supposed that she believed it all along. But now, suddenly, she saw that it had meant nothing to her.   She had obviously been trying to justify herself by works all this time, and she had not even noticed that this didn't fit with the theology she had professed.

Well, what had she thought it meant?   Faith meant belief in God and in God's graciousness toward us.   Yes, she had faith

in that sense. She was convinced that God gave her life, led
her in pleasant places, and forgave her when she did wrong.
She never worried about God's wrath or about going to hell.
She sometimes thought how much harder life would be if she
viewed the hostile, destructive forces as ultimate. She
doubted that she could dedicate herself to helping people if she
really believed that the world at its deepest level was against
that kind of service. So she found assurance in her faith in
God's graciousness, and a sense of meaningfulness in working
with God to accomplish his loving purposes. All of that was
unconscious most of the time, but she could bring it to consciousness by contrasting how she felt about things with how
she saw some other people felt—fearful of life, rejecting kind-
ness out of the belief that it could not be real, holding onto
material things as if nothing else mattered or could be trusted.
She thanked God that she was saved by faith from that.

But now she realized that all this did not justify her in her
own eyes. For that, she had to be a good Christian person.
In fact, wasn't that all the more required when one believed
that God loved one and called one to share in the divine gen-
erosity toward all creatures? It made the service easier and
more enjoyable, but it didn't make it any less important.
How could she live with herself if, recognizing God's graciousness to her, she responded with a self-centered attitude?
Well, then, how could she be "justified" by faith? What
would that even mean?

Pastor Carlstone sat glumly at his desk in his study at home.
Alice's visit had been a disaster. There had come to him,
seeking help, the finest Christian woman he knew, the most
effective worker in his church; and he had been irritated, for-
gotten everything he knew about counseling, and blurted out
silly questions. He didn't like that husband of hers, and he
resented the way Bill treated Alice when she was obviously
twice the person he was; and he supposed that was about all he
had communicated. Alice had been understandably upset
and had left in confusion.

The problem in part was that Monday was the pastor's day off, and he looked forward to Mondays as a time to relax and enjoy himself. When Alice called that Monday morning he assumed it must be a matter of great urgency. But it was only that her husband had dropped the paper on the floor. Really! Yet he knew that it *had* been a matter of great urgency to Alice, and that he had been wholly insensitive.

It had not always been like this. In his freshman year at college David Carlstone had become aware of a Christian group on campus and especially of the chaplain who led it. Chaplain Phillips, a bachelor, was a man of great intensity and great compassion. He led a frugal life, giving to the needy all he could spare—and sometimes what he could not spare. Whenever anyone on campus was in trouble, Chaplain Phillips was there offering help with no price tag attached. The group that gathered around him was the one center of active social concern on campus. Most of the students kept their distance, and so did David, but everyone respected the chaplain.

The next year David had entered a Bible study group taught by the chaplain. The topic was the teaching of Jesus. Chaplain Phillips took the teaching of Jesus with complete seriousness. He saw in it the model for the only viable way to live personally and for the only viable social order. David Carlstone had never encountered anything like this. He was a member of a church, but it had never occurred to him that the whole of life could be informed by the Christian faith. He felt now that he had to decide whether he really was a Christian or not. It was not an easy decision, but the chaplain won. David threw himself into his new faith with the same wholeheartedness as, if with less consistency than, the chaplain. He became a pacifist and a nonviolent resister of social evils. No one was surprised when he announced his intention to become a minister.

In seminary David had what he called his second conversion—from Jesus to Christ. He learned from reading

Barth that he had neglected the power of God. He had been acting as though the destiny of the world were in the hands of human beings, and all too much as if his own hands were rather specially its bearer. Now he saw that it is God who has the history of the world in his hand. That came to him with the force of revelation, all the more because it released him from pursuing the lifestyle he had learned from Chaplain Phillips, a lifestyle that had become more and more arduous. David began to relish the freedom of the Christian person. Instead of obedience to the message of Jesus he now understood Christianity to be faith in the lordship of Christ. He understood what it meant that we are saved by faith and not by works.

This enthusiasm for the sovereignty of Christ as the basis for Christian freedom went with him into his first pastorate. The people did not always understand what David Carlstone was saying, but there was something reassuring for them in their pastor's confidence. Not many came to him with personal problems, but that suited him fine. For him in those days it was the proclamation of the Word that mattered; to that and to the necessary administration of the church program he gave himself zealously. Gradually, however, doubts began to arise. There were many changes he could ring upon the one gospel, but people kept raising questions of other kinds to which he had no answer.

Matters came to a head when a fine couple brought their nineteen-year-old son to see him. It was the parents who told most of the story. The son had been their pride and joy, full of life, affectionate, intelligent, handsome. But abruptly, just a month ago, he had been expelled for homosexual acts from the church college he attended. The parents at first refused to believe the charge, but when the son admitted that he was an active homosexual, their pent-up fury turned against him. At first he fought back, but then he fell into a deep depression The parents loved their son dearly and tried to assure him that they did not reject him. They apologized for what they had said in anger. But it was too late. He had heard their contempt, confirming the contempt of so many others, and he turned it on himself. They came to Pastor Carlstone for help.

And what help had he been? He, too, had felt nothing but horror toward homosexuality. He had accepted St. Paul's comments in the Book of Romans as supporting the view that homosexuality expresses a profound theological corruption as well as being a moral evil. The pastor did not say that, but he did not say much of anything. They had a prayer together for the son's cure, and he urged the young man to go to a psychiatrist. That was about it. Two days later the young man killed himself. The mother, feeling that her harsh words had led him to this deed, was inconsolable. Pastor Carlstone tried repeatedly to see her, but she refused. Within six months she too was dead. Her husband became an alcoholic.

David Carlstone did not cease affirming the lordship of Christ, but the zeal and confidence went out of his message. He began casting about. He read avidly everything he could on homosexuality as well as on counseling. The emphasis in his sermons changed. He talked more and more about the problems of life and how to cope with them. He became widely known as a sensitive and helpful counselor. He was a greater success than ever, and he accepted the call to the much larger church where he now served. But he was no longer sure about what he was doing. In his preaching he still spoke of Christ. But he sensed that Christ was little more than a word he used to evoke pious feelings and to give authority to his own ideas. If that was where he was, what right had he to continue to be a minister of Jesus Christ?

But wasn't he being melodramatic? This morning he had failed in one counseling relationship, but surely he had succeeded in many others. The church was crowded with people who found help in his preaching. Many others were attracted to the support groups he had organized.

So many successes—all *his*! Yes, he admitted to himself, that was the way he thought about them these days. In his

Barthian years he would have never thought that. He knew then that his role was to witness to Christ. What God did with his witness was for God to decide. There had been something clean and freeing—and Christian—about that. But now, with all his sensitivity and techniques, he did think of the successes as his own—and the failures too.

The phone rang. "I need to talk with you again." The voice was that of Alice Bristol. "Of course," said David Carlstone, "I'll be delighted to see you." Perhaps the pastor would have a chance to redeem his earlier blunder.

There was a knock at the door, and as soon as he answered, Alice burst in. Before they were seated she asked, "What is justification by faith?" David broke out laughing. He had been reassured by Alice's appearance and manner that no irreparable harm had been done by his disagreeable behavior in the morning. "Twice you come to see me, Alice, once about a newspaper on the floor and now to discuss theology. In all these years you've never come before except about business. This is a red-letter day!"

Alice laughed too; the anger had gone, and she could see the humor in the situation, but she repeated the question. David was comfortably in charge now, back in the role of friendly counselor. "I could give you a lecture on Reformation doctrine, I suppose, but I don't think that's quite what you're after."

"How are *you* justified, Pastor? Is it by faith?"

David Carlstone was unnerved by this. Counselees are not supposed to demand such confidences from their counselors, and in any case, he really had no answer. He decided to give up the counseling role. After all, Alice was his equal intellectually and as a community leader. He had just been worrying about himself when she called. Maybe he should share his concern with her. He needed some counseling himself. "It's been a long time since I've put the question to myself that way, Alice, but if you mean, How can I feel good about myself? then I should say I often don't. I've been sitting here ever since you left this morning, feeling a total failure. I was just now considering whether I should leave the ministry."

Alice was stunned. She knew about the human weaknesses and doubts of ministers. She remembered the mixed bunch of students she had been with during her one year in seminary. But David Carlstone seemed different. "It's surprising how surprising I find what you've just said. You're my ideal of a pastor, and I can't picture you in any other role. But why were you so unsure of yourself this morning?"

"Frankly, Alice, what upset me was that I responded so badly to you. I'm geared to succeeding, and as long as I succeed, I don't have to worry about who I am or what I'm doing. I guess I'm justified by my successes and the appreciation I get from others. But when I fail, who and what am I? Nothing: just a failure. I was remembering this morning a time when that was different, when I knew who I was as a witness to Christ. But that doesn't fit me any longer. I look everywhere for insights and ideas—literature, science, other religions. But my search has no center. I'm not committed to anything. I don't trust anything. I'm not really a Christian."

"You know, Pastor, I don't believe you. If it were as you just now described it, your life would be going all over the place. But anyone can see by watching you that it holds together. You say you look everywhere for ideas; but when you preach, the ideas you select fit together and help people. Maybe your problem is that when you speak of Christ you still mean what you meant many years ago, whereas in your wide-spread seeking you've grown beyond that. The earlier Christ can't hold it all together, but maybe Christ is what *is* holding it *and you* together even when you don't recognize him."

"I hadn't thought of it that way," David replied, "but what you say does make sense. Most of the time I do feel good about my life, and it does seem to have some unity and direction. I guess I still mean by Christ what I used to mean. I wish I could see him in what I'm now doing, but frankly what I see is mostly myself."

"Maybe I can help, because even though you don't say much about Christ in your sermons, I've seemed to find him there. Week after week you share with us the new insight that has come to you through whatever you have been reading or experiencing. It is not new information. Sometimes I've read the books before you have and even understood them better—if you don't mind my saying so. But you put it together in a new way. That's a kind of revelation. I like to think that Christ is present in that kind of preaching."

"Thank you, Alice. You've been a Christ to me just now in the sense you are speaking of. I think you have put your finger on what my life does center on now. I am continually looking for deeper understanding of truth, especially the truth about human beings, wherever I can find it, and I do try to share it. It's odd that when you named that Christ you opened my eyes to what unifies my life, whereas I had been seeing only fragmentation."

"You've suffered a lot, I gather," Alice continued, "feeling that your quest for the light you needed to help people drew you away from Christ. If you realize that it is Christ all along whom you seek and Christ who guides you in the quest, won't you feel better about yourself and your ministry? I hope so, for especially after the way you helped me this morning I couldn't bear to think of your quitting."

"I think you are right," David mused. "But what astonishes me is that you say I helped you this morning. I spoke impatiently and abruptly, in violation of all that I knew, even at the time, I should be doing."

"Really!" Now it was Alice's turn to laugh. "So there was no profound wisdom behind your questions? Well, in any case, they stimulated me to do more serious thinking about myself than I've done for a long time. It was that thinking that brought me to the realization that I have always tried to justify myself by being good and that I'm not succeeding. That's why I want to know about justification by faith. I really can't see any way that faith has justified me or can do so. It helps make my life meaningful by assuring me that I'm working with God and that he forgives me, but as I thought about it, it seemed that believing in a loving God makes me feel the need to be good even more. And then I can't."

David reflected for a few moments. "I recall my teacher at seminary used to say that we should speak of justification by grace through faith instead of justification by faith. I wonder if it helps to emphasize grace. Maybe justification is a gift we can trust rather than a result of believing something."

"But if it's a gift," smiled Alice, "then I wish God would come across instead of leaving me to flounder this way."

"Well, maybe God has. A little while ago you spoke of seeing Christ in my preaching. I can return the favor by saying that I see grace in your life. Let's take what's going on today and look at it. This morning you became angry over something that seemed trivial to you. That could have ruined your day, and upset other people too. I blurted out something stupid that could have made things worse for you. Instead it set off a chain of thoughts that made you face yourself and brought you back to share insights I'm sure will be important to me. Now you complain that God doesn't give you anything. Well, forget for a moment about God. Something is giving you a great deal. Something is taking unpromising material and turning it into fresh insight and understanding. You've experienced this more as what's happening *to* and *in* you than as what you've done."

"So that's grace, is it?" asked Alice. "Yes, that makes sense." She paused. "I wonder what would happen if I trusted that? I've just been so preoccupied with my own virtue that I've not really been concerned about anyone else. I've been so determined to be a loving, caring, serving person that I haven't really been sensitive to what's happening in the people I'm loving. Maybe . . ."

David picked up the thought. "Maybe if I trusted grace more I would not think so much of *my* successes and *my* failures. Maybe I could think of myself as providing some of the conditions for needed change to occur without supposing that I produce the change. And maybe I could risk myself more." His mind went back to that most painful failure, when a young man in despair reached out to him—ever so slightly—and he had hidden behind a formal prayer and a useless recommendation. If he had trusted grace then . . .

"Its odd, you know," said Alice after a pause. "When we were talking about what gave unity to your life, we talked about Christ, and when we talked about what would free me from trying to justify myself, we spoke of grace. But I have an idea there's not much difference. I think the living Christ has been with me this morning, in grace and judgment. The judgment was even the most important part of the grace. Christ is life, isn't he, and I've felt very much alive through the pain as new ideas have come and old ones have fallen into new places. I'm going to start expecting Christ and trusting Christ. When I remember to do that, I don't think I'll worry so much about being a good Christian."

She rose to go. Without thinking, Pastor Carlstone bowed his head, and she in response bowed hers. "Thank you, God, for Alice Bristol," he said, and then, after a moment's pause: "And thank you, Christ, for the gift of yourself."

At the door Alice said, "Thank you, David! I'm going to tell Bill that I won't accept any longer his taking my little services for granted. He'll have to deal with me as an equal partner in the marriage. I don't know what will happen but I'm sure it will be alright."

Postscript

Chapters 2 and 3 propose a way of thinking about Christian existence that has definite implications for the life of the church in general and for pastoral care and counseling in particular. Chapters 4 and 5 offer a way of thinking about God that could guide the church's efforts to relate to the divine and could also help to renew some of our inherited Christian language. In chapters 2 and 3 the suggestions about pastoral counseling are intended to show that this understanding of Christian existence can make quite specific differences in the pastor's way of addressing people and problems. The long fictional story in chapter 5 bids to show that language about Christ and grace can arise in authentic ways when the deepest concerns of actual life are being discussed.

This is a risky kind of theology. It crosses the usual boundary between the theological bailiwick of ultimate questions and the practical problems usually reserved for psychology. It thereby presents a theological interpretation of human health and divine activity as an option within an already crowded arena. Pragmatic criteria and empirical evidence are relevant to the evaluation of such a theology, and no one can predetermine how well it will fare in this worldly competition. There is even danger that the inadequacies of a particular theological view may bring discredit upon the whole theological enterprise. Perhaps it is better for theology to speak only to the most fundamental issues, such as assurance of the worthwhileness of life, leaving the implications of this basic assurance to other disciplines.

On the other hand, it may be less dangerous to seem to identify Christian faith with the practical implications of one theological formulation than to continue to separate theology from the practical issues faced by pastors day by day. Those issues cannot be avoided, and if theology does not speak to them, pastors must turn elsewhere for help. But there are ultimate commitments inherent in the disciplines to which pastors turn, and those commitments are not always compatible with Christian faith. There arises too easily a dichotomy between the explicit Christian faith of pastors and the implicit principles by which they shape their ministry. It is time to bring this problem to focused attention and to offer an alternative. That has been the purpose of this book.

Notes

Page
22. * Roberto Assagioli, *Psychosynthesis: A Manual of Principles and Techniques* (New York: Viking Press, 1971).
25. * "The Autobiography of the Blessed Henry Suso, O. P.," in Francis MacNutt, *Healing* (Notre Dame, Ind.: Ave Maria Press, 1974), p. 66. Suso refers to himself in the third person.
27. * Norman O. Brown, *Life against Death* (Middletown, Conn.: Wesleyan University Press, 1959), chap. 16.
32. * David Hume, *Treatise of Human Nature*, Book 3, in Henry D. Aiken, ed., *Hume's Moral and Political Philosophy* (New York: Hafner, 1968). In his introduction (pp. xxiiiff.) Aiken sets this doctrine in its proper context in Hume's thought.
35. * Martin Heidegger, *Being and Time*, trans. John Macquarrie (New York: Harper & Row, 1962). The concept of authenticity is central to this book.
36. * See Edward Conze, *Buddhist Thought in India* (Ann Arbor: University of Michigan Press, 1967), pp. 132 ff.
43. * Wayne E. Oates, *Pastoral Counseling* (Philadelphia: Westminster Press, 1974), pp. 11–13.
46. * John A. T. Robinson, *Honest to God* (Philadelphia: Westminster Press, 1963), pp. 11 ff.
47. * Aristotle, *Metaphysics*, Book 1.
47. † A recent collection of Marxist writings may be found in Howard Selsam, David Goldway, and Harry Hartel, eds., *Dynamics of Social Change* (New York: International Publishers, 1970).
47. ‡ Paul Tillich, Systematic Theology (Chicago: University of Chicago Press, 1951), vol. 1, pp. 241 ff; cf. vol. 3 (1963), passim.
48. *William James, "The Dilemma of Determinism," *The Will to Believe and Other Essays in Popular Philosophy* (New York: Longmans Green, 1897).
48. † Ernst Bloch's magnum opus, *Das Prizip Hoffnung*, has not been published in English. However, he presents many of his ideas in *A Philosophy of the Future*, trans. John Cumming (New York: Herder & Herder, 1970).

48. ‡ Teilhard de Chardin, *The Phenomenon of Man*, trans. Bernard Wall (New York: Harper & Row, 1959).

48. § I have summarized Whitehead's contribution in my *A Christian Natural Theology* (Philadelphia: Westminster Press, 1965), pp. 151 ff.

59. * Albert Schweitzer, *The Quest of the Historical Jesus*, trans. W. Montgomery (New York: Macmillan, 1968), chap. 20.

60. * "The Strange New World within the Bible," a lecture given in 1916, is included in Karl Barth, *The Word of God and the Word of Man*, trans. Douglas Horton (Grand Rapids, Mich: Zondervan, 1935), pp. 28–50.

60. † Rudolf Bultmann, *Jesus and the Word*, trans. Louise Pettibone Smith and Erminie Huntress Lantero (New York: Scribner's, 1934), pp. 3–15.

60. ‡ Hans-Georg Gadamer, *Truth and Method*, trans. Garrett Barden and John Cumming (New York: Seabury Press, 1975).

Annotated Bibliography

Browning, Don S. *Atonement and Psychotherapy*. Philadelphia: Westminister Press, 1966. This shows how the acceptance required for successful therapy is grounded in an adequate doctrine of God.

Cobb, John B., Jr. *The Structure of Christian Existence*. Philadelphia: Westminster Press, 1967.

———. *God and the World*. Philadelphia: Westminster Press, 1969. These two works provide a fuller development of the theological ideas stated in the present book.

Emerson, James G., Jr. *The Dynamics of Forgiveness*. Integrated discussion of forgiveness from historical, theological, and psychological perspectives, with its application to pastoral care.

Ford, Peter S. *The Healing Trinity: Prescriptions for Body, Mind, and Spirit*. New York: Harper & Row, 1971. A physician calls for fuller use of the theological insights of the church in counseling.

James, William. *The Varieties of Religious Experience: A Study in Human Nature*. New York: Longmans, Green and Co., 1902. This classic continues to be a point of departure for both theology and psychology, and hence, indirectly, for pastoral care.

Jung, Carl G. *Psychology and Religion*. New Haven: Yale University Press, 1938. Jung's depth-psychological appreciation for theological ideas, enjoying a renewed hearing, is influencing the contemporary spiritual quest.

Lapsley, James N. *Salvation and Health: The Interlocking*

Processes of Life. Philadelphia: Westminster Press, 1972. Uses process philosophy and psychoanalytic ego psychology to develop a Christian anthropology related to pastoral ministry.

McNeill, John T. *A History of the Cure of Souls.* New York: Harper and Bros., 1954. This story of pastoral care from ancient Israel to modern times reminds us of much that we are likely to forget in our orientation to contemporary psychology.

Menninger, Karl. *Whatever Became of Sin?* New York: Hawthorn Books, 1973. A psychiatrist reviews the history of sin, shows the importance of this theological category, and urges ministers to renew the call for repentance.

Oates, Wayne E. *Protestant Pastoral Counseling.* Philadelphia: Westminster Press, 1962. Derives both the theory and practice of pastoral counseling from the Protestant pastoral heritage.

Oden, Thomas C. *Kerygma and Counseling.* Philadelphia: Westminster Press, 1966. Brings together Barth's doctrine of God's self-disclosure and the Rogerian therapy of human self-disclosure.

————. *Contemporary Theology and Psychotherapy.* Philadelphia: Westminster Press, 1967. A critical discussion of Tillich, Thurneysen, and Hiltner, and a continuing dialogue with psychotherapy based on Bonhoeffer, Teilhard, and Bultmann.

Outler, Albert C. *Psychotherapy and the Christian Message.* New York: Harper and Bros., 1954. A study of four areas of human life in which psychotherapy and Christian thought both have a stake, recognizing deep differences but calling for cooperation.

Roberts, David E. *Psychotherapy and a Christian View of Man.* New York: Scribner's, 1950. Presents theology and psychotherapy as correlative and supplementary in their view of human beings.

Rudin, Josef. *Psychotherapy and Religion.* Translated by

Elisabeth Reinecke and Paul C. Bailey. Notre Dame, Indiana: University of Notre Dame Press, 1968. Discussion of the religious meaning of Jung's depth psychology and the relation between psychotherapy and Catholic spiritual guidance.

Sherrill, Lewis Joseph. *The Struggle for the Soul.* New York: Macmillan, 1963. Traces religious development through life as the dynamic self encounters God in each stage.

Thornton, Edward E. *Theology and Pastoral Counseling.* Philadelphia: Fortress Press, 1967. Combines theological reflection about human beings with clinical reflection about theology.

Thurneysen, Eduard. *A Theology of Pastoral Care.* Richmond: John Knox Press, 1962. A pastoral theologian closely associated with Barth develops the principles of pastoral care from biblical rather than psychological sources.

Tournier, Paul. *The Meaning of Persons.* New York: Harper and Bros., 1957. One of the series of widely read books in which a physician integrates his psychiatric and theological perspectives.

Williams, Daniel Day. *The Minister and the Care of Souls.* New York: Harper & Row, 1961. A theologian reflects concretely and practically on the role and opportunities of the pastor.